To my brother Rick, his wife Lori, and their sons, Nathan and Conner

Contents

Preface vii

Acknowledgments ix

An Introduction to Problem Solving 1

   1. Ohm's Law 9

   2. Ages 17

   3. Travel by Car or Train? 21

   4. Building the Great Pyramids of Egypt 25

   5. Density 31

   6. Music 33

   7. Michael's Budget 37

Interlude I: Reading Skills 41

   8. Melting Ice 45

   9. The Speed of Light 49

  10. The Continuity Equation 53

  11. Computer Repair Calls 59

  12. Designing Computer Icons 61

  13. Traffic Lights 63

  14. Wiring Resistors in Series and in Parallel 67

  15. Genetics 77

Interlude II: Simplifying Radicals, Exponents, and Negative Exponents 83

  16. Number Puzzle 87

  17. Planning for a Nuclear Blast 89

  18. The Power Rule 95

  19. Deriving the Power Wheel 99

  20. Baseballs and the Moon 103

  21. Working with Electric Current 107

  22. The Mass of the Earth 109

Interlude III: Polynomials	115
23. Projectile Motion A	119
24. Projectile Motion B	125
25. Factoring Puzzles	131
26. Working with Capacitors: Part A	133
27. Working with Capacitors: Part B	137
28. In Search of the Wooly Mammoth	141
Interlude IV: Unit Analysis	147
29. Colors	153
30. Semi-conductors	159
31. Who Is the Homerun King?	163
32. HIV and the AIDS Virus	167
33. How Warm Is It? Fahrenheit and Celsius	171
34. Global Warming and the Ozone	177
Interlude V: Trigonometry	183
35. Billboard	189
36. Fiber Optics	193
37. Lightning and..........Thunder	201
38. Alternating Current	205
39. Independent Electronics Research	209
40. Impedance and Trigonometry	211
Appendix A: Drawing Skill Opportunities	219
Appendix B: MathPro	237
Glossary	241

Preface

This text is written specifically for you, a technology student, as an introduction to problem solving. Because technology changes daily, an education that focuses exclusively on memorizing technological facts would not prepare you for long term success in the job market. What does have longevity in an ever-changing workplace, however, is the ability to solve problems.

This book consists of 40 different Thought Projects that cover a wide range of topics and require a variety of different problem solving skills. Because rote memorization is the enemy of true problem solving, the projects have been constructed in a variety of forms. In some, the problem statement is at the beginning, while in others, several pages of introductory material must be read before the problem statement is given. Many of the projects contain additional skill levels that extend either the problem solving technique used for that project, or provide an opportunity for you to delve deeper into the topic. Additionally, the level of required reading increases as you work through the book. To be an effective problem solver, you must be comfortable confronting problems of a type that you have never before encountered and that may feature unfamiliar language and terminology.

Regardless of the topic, or the skill level, all of the projects in the book have one thing in common—they can be approached using Polya's four-step problem solving strategy. Although it might not be readily apparent in some cases, this technique, which is discussed in the Introduction, can be applied to all of the Thought Projects contained in the book.

Polya's process involves four key steps:

I. Understand the Problem
II. Devise a Plan
III. Carry out the Plan
IV. Look Back

Each Thought Project is broken into these four steps. Questions are asked to guide you through the process and to help you develop sound strategies for tackling the problems. The worktext format of this text is designed to allow you to write directly in the book itself.

A number of features are built into the text to provide you with extra help and guidance, they include:

Math Review

Each Thought Project includes one, or more, marginal Math Review boxes to direct you to the pertinent math coverage in the *Tools for Problem Solving* text. You will derive the greatest benefit from this text by getting in the habit of turning to Part V of your Tools book whenever you need to review or learn a math skill. The Math Review box tells you exactly which section of the book will be of most help. In addition, it guides you to the corresponding section in the **MathPro** software. Spending time on MathPro will allow you to develop and practice the math skills that you will need for this, and subsequent, courses at ITT Technical Institute. A brief introduction to MathPro is presented in Appendix B.

Problem Solving Tips

Another boxed feature that appears in the margin of selected Thought Projects is one that provides problem solving tips. This box is integrated, as appropriate, to offer suggestions and insights into the various kinds of strategies you may employ to solve a particular problem.

Drawing Skill Opportunities

Selected Thought Projects lend themselves to acquiring another set of technical skills that will be useful to CAD students. Where appropriate a Drawing Skill Opportunity appears as the last component of the Thought Project. These "opportunities" provide a link to the step-by-step keystroke Actrix commands presented in Appendix A.

If you spend time working through each assigned Thought Project and make optimal use of the reference tools provided, you will be on the road to becoming a skilled problem solver and a highly marketable employee in the technology sector.

Logos

The opening page for each Thought Process includes a logo that identifies the Thought Project's primary application. Some Thought Projects have more than one application. When that is the case, both logos are included within the project. The text uses four logos. They are:

 General Interest

 Electronics

 Science

 CAD/Drawing

Acknowledgments

I would like to thank the many people who made this book possible. I am indebted to the publisher, a team effort on the part of Pearson Custom Publishing and Prentice Hall, and their staffs for assistance in both the development and production processes. In particular, I would like to extend my thanks to Frank Burrows for his counsel, advice, and sound insights.

I would also like to thank ITT/ESI's corporate curriculum managers. Tom Bledsaw, Wen Liu, Bill Perkins, and Andrea Worrell, under the leadership of Sunand Bhattacharya, spent many hours and months brainstorming and planning the shape of the new curriculum and the approach of its textual components. Without their vision, this book would not have been possible.

Special thanks goes to all of the ITT/ESI faculty members who have so graciously given of their spare time to make suggestions, review material, and offer support for this project. Your dedication to your profession changes the lives of our students daily. A special thanks also goes to Eric Stimmel for the quality of the artwork in the text and the speed with which he produced it.

Lastly, my largest debt of gratitude goes to my editor, Ann Heath, for her superb editorial assistance, unflagging support, and unwavering dedication to the production of quality educational materials for the students of ITT Technical Institute.

Brian K. Saltzer
Pittsburgh, PA

An Introduction to Problem Solving

Most of us use the word "problem" in our daily conversation. We say things like

- "I'm having a problem getting on-line."
- "The problem is that we just don't communicate."
- "I had a problem finding a parking space."

Many of the problems we encounter are easily solved, but others require a more thoughtful approach. The challenge that confronts us in this text is to develop a broad-based problem solving strategy and a set of skills that will allow us to solve a variety of complex problems. Once we are comfortable with the steps in problem solving, we will see that the process is basically the same regardless of the nature of the problem. We will learn how to solve problems as diverse as:

- Finding the power dissipated across a resistor in an electric circuit
- Determining the amount of time it takes for light from a supernova to reach earth
- Analyzing the information on a string of DNA

Pólya's Four-Step Process

The broad problem solving method that we will study is based on the work of the mathematician and educator, George Pólya. He was the first person to formalize a problem solving strategy that is broad enough to encompass all types of problems. This strategy, usually referred to as *Pólya's four-step process*, exploits the underlying similarities that all problems share.

    I.   Understand the problem

    II.   Devise a plan

    III. Carry out the plan

    IV. Look back

George Pólya 20th century mathematician/educator who formalized a four-step problem solving strategy.

Copyright © Associated Press

The problems to which we can apply Pólya's four steps can be broken into two distinct sets—technical and non-technical. Because the problem solving method and its application to non-technical problems will be covered in your *Dynamics in an Information Society* course, our focus in this text will be primarily on problems of a technical nature.

Because our goal is to learn to apply this four-step strategy to real world problems, it is important to become familiar with each stage in the process.

I. UNDERSTAND THE PROBLEM

The first step is the most important. If we do not understand the problem that confronts us, we have no hope of finding a solution. A lack of understanding can prevent us from beginning to work on the problem, or worse, lead us down a dead end path. Because the understanding of language and terminology is the most important part of the problem solving process, an entire section on reading comprehension has been included in your problem solving tools book.

This first of Pólya's steps has four major components that must be addressed regardless of the type of problem that confronts us:

a) Do we understand all of the words/terminology in the problem?

b) What is the exact problem that we are being asked to solve?

c) Is there enough information given for us to solve the problem?

d) Is there extraneous information given in the problem that can be eliminated from the problem solving process?

II. DEVISE A PLAN

During this stage we begin to develop a strategy that will yield the solution to the problem. The following is a list of some useful tactics to employ:

a) Draw a picture

b) Make a model

c) Look for any patterns or trends

d) Do an experiment

e) Gather statistics that relate to the problem

f) Construct an equation that associates quantities that relate to the problem

Because this text focuses mainly on solving problems of a more technical nature, we may find the last three items in the list to be the most helpful.

III. CARRY OUT THE PLAN

In Step III, we execute the strategy devised in Step II. It is important for the problem solver to be open to any and all results. The strategy attempted may be 100 percent correct, 0 percent correct, or anywhere in between.

Remember that any result, whether positive or negative, is simply more information for us to feed back into step II!

Because the strategies of performing an experiment, gathering related statistics, and constructing an equation are very useful in solving problems of a technical nature, let's take time and discuss what is involved in carrying out each of them.

DO AN EXPERIMENT The word *experiment* may be slightly misleading and restrictive for our purposes. We do not necessarily mean an experiment as in a science lab with test tubes and bunsen burners. Rather, a better way for us to think about this tactic is "to do something physical" or "to take a physical measurement." The problem solving strategy that we choose may indeed be a chemistry experiment, but it can just as easily be wiring an electronic circuit or sitting at a computer and using a drafting software package. In other words, when we consider using experimentation as a problem solving technique, we must use the word "*experiment*" as broadly as possible.

GATHER STATISTICS Just as with experimentation, it is advantageous for us to think about statistics and the manner in which we gather them in a broad context. Our statistics might be pages and pages of numerical data that need to be graphed in order to yield effective information or one or two facts that relate to the problem. Similarly, our methods of acquiring statistics can range from physically taking a survey to accessing the information via the Internet. In the simplest form, we can think of statistics as being *facts* that relate to the problem.

CONSTRUCT AN EQUATION This technique is a powerful tool for solving technical problems. However, to use this strategy effectively we must be able to manipulate the equation. If we cannot work with the equation, we will not be able to extract the information required to solve the problem. Because using equations and mathematics will often be the most efficient problem solving technique for the Thought Projects in this text, we have developed extensive materials to assist in acquiring the mathematical skills that are necessary.

Mathematical instruction and support are provided in your *Tools for Problem Solving* text and in the *MathPro* software that accompanies it. Part V of your Tools book includes explanations, examples, and exercises to help gain the mathematical skills needed. The instructor will suggest exercises that will be helpful for each Thought Project. MathPro software provides guided instruction, including video clips, and a wealth of exercises for practice.

> **Math Review**
>
> Math Review Notes are placed throughout the book to guide you to the appropriate section in your Tools book and in MathPro.

IV. LOOK BACK

The final stage of Pólya's process asks us to evaluate the effectiveness of the problem solving strategy we used. Some of the questions that we need to ask are:

- Is our answer the full solution or only a partial one?
- Is our answer correct?
- If confronted with this problem (or a problem of a similar type) again, would we use the same problem solving strategy or modify it in some way?

Now let's practice applying Pólya's four steps to the following simple problem statement:

Problem:

How many circles with a radius of 1 inch can we fit in a rectangle that is 2 feet long and 1 foot wide?

I. UNDERSTAND THE PROBLEM

This problem statement provides a wonderful example of why it is important to understand the exact question we are being asked to solve. At first glance, this statement seems to be a very simple problem that will not require any elaborate problem solving techniques. However, upon closer analysis, we see that this problem does not lend itself to a single, unique solution. There are at least three different ways that we can interpret the problem:

a) Because the problem statement does not say that the circles cannot overlap, we could place an infinite number of them in the rectangle. This answer would be a reasonable solution to the stated problem.

b) Another interpretation is that we want to determine how many circles could be placed into the rectangle if the circles are placed edge-to-edge, but do not overlap. A problem solving strategy addressing that problem would be an acceptable solution to the problem statement as written.

c) Finally, we could interpret the problem statement as requesting that we compare the area of the rectangle to the area of the circle. Using mathematics, we could simply divide the area of the rectangle by the area of one circle. In that case our result would probably not be an integer as in interpretation *b*.

Because there are several different options depending on how we interpret the problem statement, we are now faced with a decision. Do we solve the problem in its current form, including all of the different interpretations, or do we want to reword the problem so that it has a unique solution?

To further illustrate Pólya's four steps in our example, let's reword the problem so that it has a unique solution:

Problem:

How many circles with a radius of 1 inch can we fit into a rectangle that is 2 feet long and 1 foot wide if no circles are allowed to overlap or protrude outside of the box?

This new problem statement is now clear and has one distinct solution. Our next task involves Step II. of Pólya's process.

II. DEVISE A PLAN

There are several different strategies that we can employ to solve the problem. Some of these strategies include:

a) Draw a full-sized representation of the problem by hand and physically draw in the circles.

b) Draw a smaller version of the problem to scale and manually insert the circles until we reach the solution.

c) Use a drafting software package to make a drawing of the problem to scale and use the same methods as *a* and *b*.

d) Use mathematical reasoning to decide how many circles will fit without making a drawing of the problem.

e) Use a combination of the strategies.

The decision of which strategy to implement is largely one of preference and ability. First, we must judge those skills that we already possess or are willing to acquire. Do we have access to the tools to make a hand drawing to scale? Do we have access to a drafting software package that will allow us to make the drawing? If we have access to the software, do we have the necessary software skills to solve the problem? Do we have the necessary mathematical background to choose strategy *d*? Will one strategy solve the problem faster than the others?

Once we have decided which problem solving technique is the most efficient to use, we must carry out the strategy.

III. CARRY OUT THE PLAN

To illustrate our four step process most effectively, we will choose a problem solving strategy that does not require the use of a software package or other tools. To illustrate this third step in the problem solving method, let's use mathematics as our problem solving approach (strategy *d*).

Math Review

For a review of the geometry concepts presented in this problem, consult your Tools book.

Read: Appendix A.2, A.3.

Notice that even though we have chosen mathematics as our strategy, it still may be helpful to make a sketch of the problem:

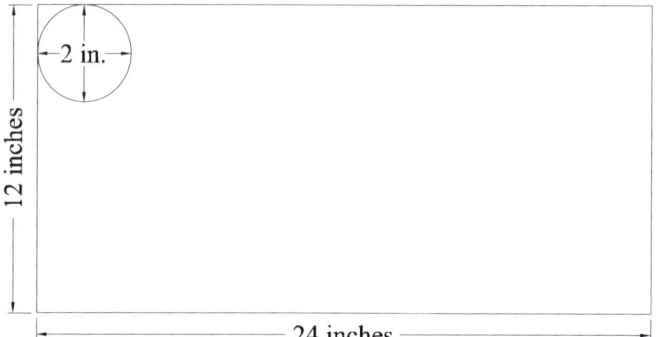

Figure 1.1

Notice that in Figure 1.1 we have expressed the dimensions of the rectangle in inches so that we can more easily compare it to the circles which are also shown in inches.

Using mathematics, we see that because our circles have a radius of 1 inch, they are 2 inches across at their widest point.

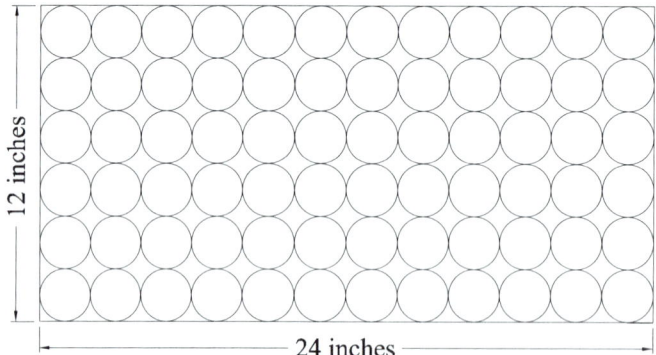

Figure 1.2

Using mathematical reasoning and our drawing, we see (Figure 1.2) that we can place six rows of 12 circles in the rectangle. We can now find the number of circles in the rectangle by either adding them, or by multiplying 12 times 6. We conclude that 72 circles can fit in the rectangle.

IV. LOOK BACK

During the last phase of Pólya's method, we evaluate the effectiveness of our strategy. Some of the questions that we should ask include:

a) Is our answer a correct solution to the problem?

b) Can this strategy be applied to other problems of a similar type?

c) Can this strategy be extended to the original problem statement that we reworded?

d) Is there any error attached to our solution? If so, is there a way to quantify this error?

e) If confronted with this problem again, would we use the same strategy, a modified version of it, or choose a totally different one?

Ok, now it's your turn! This book contains Thought Projects from a variety of real-world situations. Because rote memorization is the enemy of true problem solving, the projects are written in a variety of forms and include many different reading and skill levels. Sometimes the problem to solve is given at the beginning of the project. Other times you will need to read several pages of background material before you are given the problem to solve. In some cases only the required information is given, in others excess information is given and you must sift through it to extract what is necessary and applicable. You may choose to do research on the Internet, perform a physical experiment, use mathematics, or employ a number of other strategies to solve the problem. As you become more adept at problem solving, you may not consciously think about each of Pólya's steps; however, they are always at work in the background. At the end of the course, you should have acquired problem solving skills that will help you excel at ITT Technical Institute and in your future career.

DRAWING SKILL OPPORTUNITY 1: DRAWING CIRCLES IN A RECTANGLE

In addition to systematically working through an application of Pólya's four-step problem solving process, the topic of circles and squares allows us to introduce another facet of the book. As you look through the book, you will notice that some of the Thought Projects are identified with an icon to indicate that a Drawing Skill Opportunity is available.

Rather than offering additional problem solving strategies, these skill opportunities provide a platform for introducing a particular skill using a software package. Turn to Appendix A to find the sample Actrix Commands that accompanies this introduction to problem solving.

Thought Project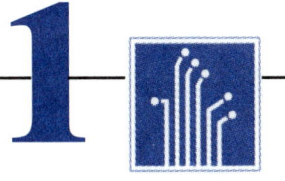

 Ohm's Law

1

Electricity plays such an important role in our society that it is hard to imagine life without it. Amazingly, electricity and its ever-present companion, magnetism, is a very recent discovery when compared to the time that human beings have walked on earth. Although we have evidence that the ancient Egyptians used lodestones (a natural form of magnet), our modern understanding of electricity and magnetism traces its roots to the work of such 18th/19th century scientists as Andre Ampere and Georg Ohm. It was their thoughtful and creative experiments that led to our current understanding of electrical circuits and electronics.

At the heart of electricity and electronics is the concept of a **circuit**.

> A **circuit** is a complete, closed path that allows electricity to flow. If there is a break in the path there will be no flow of electricity.

This flow of electricity is usually referred to as *electric current*. Electrical current can be pictured in the same way that we picture the current in a stream. Just as a greater current in a stream implies that more water is passing by a certain point on the shore, more electrical current implies that more electricity is passing by a certain point in the circuit. Because of his major contributions to this field of study, electrical current is named for Andre Ampere. The unit of Amperes is usually shortened to the simpler form of *Amps*.

In the same way that some force, like gravity, must cause water to flow in the first place, something must cause the electricity to flow. All circuits have a battery or some other device that exerts a pressure that causes the current flow. This electrical pressure is known as **voltage** after Alessandro Volta (1745–1827).

> **Voltage**, or voltage source, can be thought of as electrical pressure. It is this electrical pressure, or voltage, that causes the current to flow when the switch is closed in the circuit. Voltage is measured in Volts.

Skill Level

I

Andre Ampere (1775–1836) French physicist/mathematician who helped to lay the foundations for modern electromagnetic theory.

Copyright © Leonard de Selva/CORBIS

However, the current flow that is caused by the voltage source does not appear without opposition. The amount of this opposition depends upon the type of material through which the current must flow. Some materials allow electricity to flow more readily than others. Those materials that allow for a large current flow are known as *conductors*, while those materials that inhibit flow are known as *insulators*. This opposition to current flow is known as *resistance* and is measured in units of Ohms. This unit is usually expressed using the capital Greek letter omega: Ω.

Problem:

How much voltage would be required to cause .005 Amps of current to flow through a 1KΩ resistor?

I. UNDERSTAND THE PROBLEM

Read the problem statement carefully. Do you understand all of the terms used?

Problem Solving Tips

If you do not understand the terms used, reread the background information on electricity and highlight the terms that are used in the problem statement.

II. DEVISE A PLAN

a) What are some strategies that you may use to solve this problem?

b) What are the advantages and disadvantages of each of the strategies you listed in *a*?

c) Are any special skills required to implement any of the strategies?

III. CARRY OUT THE PLAN

Although there are a variety of strategies available, the two most effective are:

1) Physically construct the circuit and take a measurement of the voltage.

2) Use mathematics to solve the problem.

Strategy 1: Physical Construction of the Circuit

At this point, your instructor will give an introduction to the equipment and materials necessary for this problem solving strategy.

d) Draw a picture (schematic) of the circuit you will construct.

e) How do you plan to measure the voltage? Discuss the technique/strategy that you are planning to use.

f) Repeat the experiment three times. What voltage was measured?

   Trial 1:

   Trial 2:

   Trial 3:

g) How did your measured value compare with others in your class? If there was a difference, what might be some reasons for it?

h) Did this problem solving technique of physically constructing the circuit have any drawbacks that you did not expect? Explain.

Strategy 2: Using Mathematics

Using the language of mathematics, it is possible to write a mathematical sentence that relates voltage, current, and resistance. This mathematical sentence takes the form of an *equation*. An equation is a mathematical statement that says, "Even though the left side of the equation and the right side of the equation may look different, they have the same value."

An equation may contain only numbers:

$$\frac{1}{2} = .5 \qquad \text{Equation 1}$$

letters:

$$ab = cd \qquad \text{Equation 2}$$

or a mixture of both:

$$3x + 5y = 2z \qquad \text{Equation 3}$$

In all cases, however, each mathematical sentence is saying that the terms on the left side of the equal sign have the same value as the terms on the ride side. It is important to note that the letters in Equations 2 and 3 obey the same rules as do the numbers. Letters used in equations are called *variables* and represent a number that we do not know.

i) Write out, in words, what Equation 2 and Equation 3 say mathematically.

Using the language of equations, we can express the relationship between the three quantities in our circuit as:

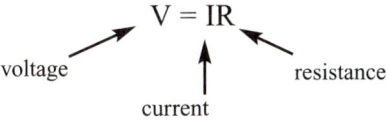

This equation is commonly called "Ohm's Law." In words, Ohm's Law says:

"The voltage is equal to the current multiplied by the resistance."

Math Review

Read: Section 1.2

MathPro: 1.2B

For an overview of MathPro see Appendix B in this book.

Georg Ohm (1775–1836)
German physicist who formulated a law relating voltage, current, and resistance known as "Ohm's Law," which is central to the study of electricity.

Courtesy of the Library of Congress

Notice that even though there is no multiplication sign between the I and the R, their placement next to one another implies that they are to be multiplied.

j) Given Ohm's Law, how can we use mathematics to solve our problem?

k) Using Ohm's Law, how much voltage would be required to solve our problem?

IV. LOOK BACK

l) Were you able to use both problem solving strategies with equal ease? If not, why not?

m) Was the solution to the problem the same using both strategies? If not, by how much did they differ?

n) If the two solutions were different, what might explain the difference?

o) If you were to encounter this problem again, would you modify either of these techniques? If so, how?

DRAWING SKILL OPPORTUNITY 2: DRAWING A SIMPLE CIRCUIT

Ohm's Law, and the framework of the simple circuit that accompanies it, provides us with a wonderful opportunity to learn another set of technical skills that will be useful in the vocational field. An alternate approach to solving the circuit mathematically, or wiring the circuit and taking a physical measurement, is to use one of the more popular drafting software packages. By learning a software package, we equip ourselves with a powerful tool with which to visualize problems and physical situations.

In this Thought Project, we learned about both resistors and direct current voltage sources. The Drawing Skill that accompanies this module is an introduction to the commands necessary to draw the circuit that we created in this Thought Project.

If you are interested in learning the Drawing Skill that accompanies this module, your instructor will introduce you to the appropriate commands. As an additional resource, a detailed explanation of both the necessary commands and their order is given in Appendix A.

Thought Project

Ages

In Thought Project 1, we solved a long, more complex problem that involved careful reading and analysis. Some problems, like the one presented here, are more straightforward.

Skill Level

Problem:

An eight-year old boy named Nathan wants to compare his age with that of his mother and his grandfather. His mother is exactly four times his age and his grandfather is exactly seven times his age. How old is Nathan's mother? How old is his grandfather?

I. UNDERSTAND THE PROBLEM

a) Underline the key pieces of information contained in the problem statement.

- Nathan is 8
- his mother is exactly for times his age
- his grandfather is exactly 7 times his age

18   Thought Project 2

Math Review

Read: Section 1.2B
MathPro: 1.2B

II. DEVISE A PLAN

b) Can you rewrite the problem statement in the form of an equation? If so, what is required for you to write it?

$$8 \times 4 = 32$$
$$8 \times 7 = 56$$
$$N = 8$$
$$4N = \text{Mother's age}$$
$$7N = \text{Grandfather's age}$$
$$4(8) = \text{Mother}$$
$$7(8) = \text{Grandfather}$$

c) Can the mother's age be found using the same problem solving strategy as the one used for finding the grandfather's age? Explain. yes. All you have to do is multiply the age of the boy by however many times older the grandfather is.

III. CARRY OUT THE PLAN

d) Solve the equations. How old is Nathan's mother? How old is his grandfather? Nathan's mother - 32
Grandfather - 56

e) One year from now, will the same relationship exist between Nathan's age and that of his mother and his grandfather? Use numbers to illustrate your answer.

Nathan = 9
Mother = 33
Grandfather = 57

9 · 4 = 36
9 · 7 = 63

Dosen't work.

IV. LOOK BACK

f) How does solving this problem using an equation differ from the one used in the Ohm's Law example?

Skill Level

Problem:

Nathan has two brothers, Conner and Josh. If we add 2 to Conner's age, it is exactly 1/2 the age of their older brother Josh who is 12. How old is Conner?

Math Review

Read: Section 1.2
MathPro: 1.2D

Show your work.

Nathan = 8
Conner = 4
Josh = 12

Josh = 12 − 6 = 6 is ½ of 12

6 − 2 = (4 = Conners age)

Thought Project 3

Travel by Car or Train?

Problem:

Bob Rodriguez, the Albany, NY sales representative for Advanced Drafting Software, Inc., must attend the regional sales meeting in New York City. Unfortunately, his car is in the shop so he must make other travel arrangements to get there. One option is to take a train that departs at 8 A.M. the following day. Alternatively, he could ride to the meeting with another sales rep.

Bob has an important presentation to deliver at the meeting and needs to arrive as early as possible. He knows that the train travels at 80 miles an hour, but has a one-half hour layover halfway through the 156 mile trip. He also is aware of the fact that his friend cannot depart before 8 A.M. and will adamantly refuse to drive any faster than 55 miles per hour.

If both methods of transportation leave at the same time (8 A.M.) will the train or the car allow him to reach the regional sales meeting sooner?

I. UNDERSTAND THE PROBLEM

a) What are the key pieces of information in this problem?

Train - leave 8 A.M - Traveling 8 m.p.h.
½ hr. layover

Car leave 8.AM 55 m.p.h.
Overall 156 miles

II. DEVISE A PLAN

b) Is there a way to make a drawing of this problem? If so, how?

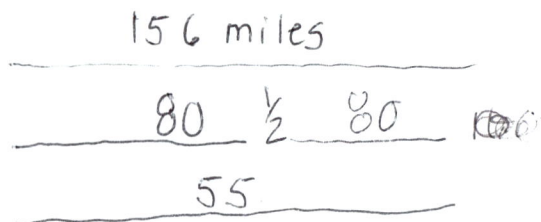

c) Is it possible to break this problem into smaller pieces in order to solve it? How?

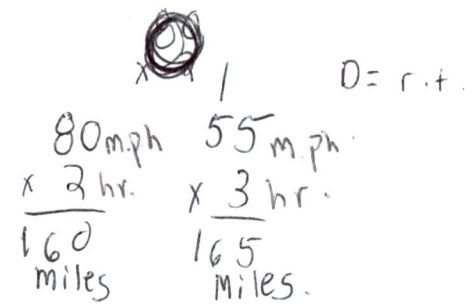

d) Discuss your strategy for solving this problem.

If you travel by train it will take an overall 2½ hrs. with the ½ hr layover to travel 160 miles.

By car it will take 3 hrs. to drive 165 miles

Divide and Round 156 ÷ 80
Divide and Round. 156 ÷ 55.

(See how many times 80 will go into 156 and how many times 55 will go into 156 then that will give you how many miles each vehicle traveled then add the ½ hr. layover to the train and you got your answer.

III. CARRY OUT THE PLAN

e) Execute your strategy and determine which method of travel would allow Bob to reach the meeting in the shortest amount of time.

Distance = 156 miles

Train	Car
80 m.p.h.	55 m.p.h.
(80×2) in 2 hrs. = 160 miles	(55×2) = 110 miles
w/ ½ hr layover (2½ hrs.)	Too short in 3 hrs, 165 miles

The Train is FASTER

IV. LOOK BACK

f) How efficient was the strategy you used? Would your strategy be useful for solving other types of problems? Explain.

The strategy was very efficient because all I had to do was take the speed to see how many m.p.h each means of transportation was going and then I added the ½ hr layover to the train. and rounded the time it took to travel 156 miles.

My strategy would definetly work at solving problems like this and various other problems anything that requires multiplying and dividing numbers to find an objective number, it won't fail.

Math Review

Read: Section 1.2
MathPro: 1.2D

Thought Project

Building the Great Pyramids of Egypt

Standing in the Nile Valley are structures that remind us daily of the ingenuity and technical abilities of our ancestors. The pyramids of ancient Egypt both awe and baffle modern engineers who wonder, "How did they do it?" How did an ancient civilization that did not yet have the mathematical tools of calculus, or modern hydraulic equipment, build structures so architecturally sound that even today we cannot slide a piece of paper between the blocks?

While the pyramids of ancient Egypt are the most well known, there are other examples of pyramids in other regions of the world, most notably Central America.
Courtesy of PhotoDisc, Inc.

Problem:

Setting: Time: 3000 B.C.
Place: Lower Egypt

Situation: You and your team are the recently appointed structural engineers for the current Pharaoh.

Using only those materials and equipment available in the time of the Pharaohs, devise a plan to build a pyramid.

I. UNDERSTAND THE PROBLEM

a) What are some key pieces of information that are required to solve this problem?

Skill Level

26 Thought Project 4

b) Identify some resources for obtaining the necessary information.

c) Based on what you know about the land of the Pharaohs, what are possible strategies for building a pyramid?

Contrary to popular opinion, influenced largely by Hollywood movies, the pyramids were not built by row after row of slaves who dragged enormous rocks for miles across the sand. Writings from the period show that the pyramids were actually national monuments in which the citizens took great pride. These records document the fact that a large portion of the physical labor was actually completed by Egyptian farmers during those times when the Nile River flooded. The annual floods were a great blessing because they provided the irrigation and fertilization required to grow crops. Because the flooded land was impossible to farm for several months each year, the farmers were available for pyramid construction.

II. DEVISE A PLAN

d) Does this information about the annual flooding of the Nile suggest any modifications to your original strategies for building the pyramids?

A map of the Nile Delta region of Egypt. It was the flooding of the Nile that allowed for the large stones to be moved great distances by flotation.

Hint
Look at the work done by Blaise Pascal and Archimedes.

e) If you modified your original problem solving strategy after researching the hint about Archimedes' or Pascal's Principle, are there now any additional pieces of information that you need to complete your strategy?

III. CARRY OUT THE PLAN

f) Write out the equations that are known as Archimedes' Principle and Pascal's Principle.

g) Write out what each letter in each of the equations represents.

Archimedes:

Pascal:

Archimedes (c. 287–212 B.C.)
Greek mathematician/physicist who created geometric techniques for finding areas and volumes of difficult figures.

Courtesy of Alinari/Art Resource, NY

Math Review

If you need a refresher on equations and variables, you can find these topics in your Tools for Problem Solving Text:

Read: Section 1.2
MathPro: Section 1.2B

Blaise Pascal (1623–1662)
French mathematician/physicist who pioneered work on calculating devices and probability theory.

Courtesy of Giraudon/Art Resource, NY

h) Do these two principles suggest any possibilities for your original problem solving strategies?

i) Using real world numbers, show how the two principles can be used to assist you in your pyramid building effort.

IV. LOOK BACK

j) What did your research and the discovery of new information teach you? Based on that information, what is your final suggestion for the problem solving strategy for this Thought Project?

Skill Level II

Problem:

Explain how Pascal's Principle applies to automobile brakelines.

Skill Level III

Problem:

Identify resources, carry out the research, and give a reasonable physical explanation for another architectural challenge—Stonehenge.

DRAWING SKILL OPPORTUNITY 3: DRAWING TRIANGLES

In this Drawing Skill opportunity, we will learn how to construct an image of the front face of one of the pyramids that we addressed in this Thought Project. Picture in your mind's eye the many different views of a pyramid that we can use. If we look top down on the pyramid, the image that we see is a square:

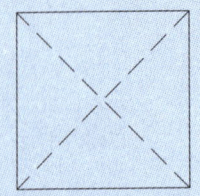

Alternately, we can view the pyramid with one of the faces as our frontal view. In this case, our image is a triangle:

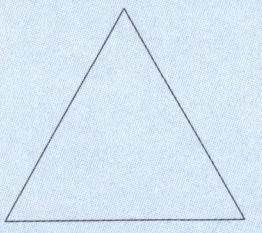

This Drawing Skill opportunity concerns the latter view. Your instructor will guide you through the rest of the project.

A detailed listing of the necessary commands to generate the front view of the pyramid are given in Appendix A.

Thought Project 5
Density

Did you know that diamonds and the graphite in your pencil are made of the same thing? Even though they look very different and have very different physical properties, they are both made of carbon. How tightly the atoms of carbon are packed together determines the physical characteristics of the object. We call this atomic tightness *density*.

The density of a material (usually expressed using the lower case Greek letter rho, ρ) is defined as the mass of the material divided by its volume. The equation for density is

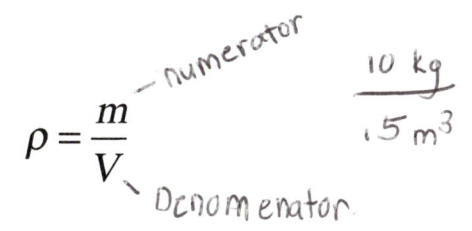

$$\rho = \frac{m}{V}$$

(handwritten annotations: "numerator" pointing to m, "Denomenator" pointing to V, and $\frac{10 \text{ kg}}{.5 \text{ m}^3}$)

Skill Level: I

Math Review
It may be helpful to review the coverage of fractions in your Tools book.
Read: Section R2
MathPro: R2 A, B

Problem:

Find the density of a material that has a mass of 10 Kg and a volume of .5 m³.

I. UNDERSTAND THE PROBLEM

a) What is the numerator of this expression?

   m = 10 kg

b) What is the denominator of this expression?

   V = .5 m³

II. CARRY OUT THE PLAN (Solve the Problem)

c) What is the density of the material?

d) How are the units of the density found?

Make .5 a whole number 5, then make 10 – 10.0 – which is a 100 then dive 5 into a hundred which would be 20.

III. LOOK BACK

e) How is the density affected by increasing the mass while holding the volume constant?

f) How is the density affected by increasing the volume while holding the mass constant?

Problem Solving Tips

With simple problems such as this one, steps in the problem solving process may be combined.
In this problem you do not have to *Devise a Plan* since the strategy "use an equation" is given to you. Therefore you may go directly to solving the problem.

Thought Project 6
Music

Composers have many tools at their disposal to produce different musical effects. Among the most important tools are the *measures*, *beats*, and *note values* the composer uses.

A *measure* is a way of dividing time by grouping beats and it often takes hundreds of measures to make up a musical work. Each measure contains a certain allowed number of beats. The number of beats in a measure is arbitrarily determined by the composer.

A *note value* is the duration of a single tone or discrete musical event (like a single strike on a drum). A *beat* is a unit of measurement of the division of time in music and is indicated in choral or orchestral music by the motions of the conductor's hand or baton. In notation, the beat is given a certain note value and the beats are further subdivided by smaller note values. Conventional note values are: whole note, half note, quarter note, eighth note, sixteenth note, etc. Each of the values after the whole note are relative to the duration of the whole note. For example, the eighth note is $1/8^{th}$ the duration of the whole note.

Skill Level I

Problem:

If 5 quarter notes and 6 eighth notes are added together, how many whole notes result?

I. UNDERSTAND THE PROBLEM

a) How would you attack this problem?

$$\frac{10}{8} \quad \frac{5}{4} \quad + \quad \frac{6}{8} \quad \frac{16}{8}$$

34 Thought Project 6

II. DEVISE A PLAN

b) Write a fractional expression that will help solve the problem.

$$\frac{10}{8} \quad \frac{5}{4} + \frac{6}{8} = \frac{16}{8} = 2$$

Math Review

It may be helpful to review the coverage of fractions in your Tools book.

Read: Section R.2

MathPro: R.2 A, B

III. CARRY OUT THE PLAN

c) Solve the problem and show your work.

$$\frac{10}{8} \quad \frac{5}{4} + \frac{6}{8} = \frac{16}{8} \quad 8\overline{)16} = 2$$

IV. LOOK BACK

d) What general statement can you make about adding fractions?

Find a common denominator make sure you reduce

To achieve a very different rhythmic feel, composers often employ a pattern called a two-beat triplet. This triplet consists of three notes. These notes are shortened so that together the three notes occupy only two total instead of the normal three. Obviously, this type of pattern divides time differently than does the basic pattern of half notes, etc.

Skill Level

II

Problem:

How many sets of two beat triplets could fit into five measures of a score if each measure is allowed to have four total beats?

Show your work.

5 × 2 = 10

Skill Level III

Rank the following from most total beats to fewest total beats:

a) 15 quarter notes   15

b) 8 half notes   16

c) 6 sets of two-beat triplets   12

d) 9 whole notes   36

Thought Project 7

Michael's Budget

[handwritten:]
23,400 yr.
17,340 - in bill yr.
6,060 Left over yr.
116.54 weekly

Problem:

Upon completion of his degree at ITT Technical Institute, Michael is hired as a technician at the rate of $900 every 2 weeks (after taxes). His monthly bills are:

Rent	$500
Electricity	80
Gas heat	65
Car payment	300
Car insurance	70
Fuel for car	80
Groceries	150
Credit cards	200

Given Michael's current expenses, how much money is available weekly for leisure spending?

I. UNDERSTAND THE PROBLEM

a) Do you have all of the information you need to solve this problem? If not, what additional information do you need? *[handwritten:]* No, you need to know

Skill Level I

II. DEVISE A PLAN

b) What steps do you need to take to solve this problem?

you need to look at his current Salary then subtract his current expenses then that will give you his current total for leisure spending

c) Is mathematics an appropriate strategy to use in solving this problem? Explain. Defintely important Math is without subtrating his expenses from his salary you cannot find the answer.

d) Do you need to find an equation to solve this problem? Explain your reasoning.

III. CARRY OUT THE PLAN

e) Solve the problem. How much money will Michael have left over each week after paying his bills?

```
rent = 500           $900
Electricity = 80      ×3
Gas/heat = 65        500
Car payment = 300    300
Car Insurance = 70   200
Fuel for car = 80    150
Groceries = 150       80
Credit cards = 200    80
                      70
                      65
                    -----
                    1445
```

f) Suppose that Michael's electric and home gas bills were due on the 15th of the month instead of the 1st. How would this different information affect the problem?

g) What effect, if any, would the different payment date have on your answer?

Thought Project 7

Skill Level II

Problem:

Instead of spending his additional earnings each month, Michael chose to open a savings account offering 3 percent interest accrued monthly. Calculate the amount of money in his savings account at the end of each of the following periods:

a) At the end of three months

b) At the end of six months

c) At the end of the first year

Math Review
Read: Section 2.7
MathPro: 2.7A, B

116.54 × 4 weeks (1 month) = 466.16 / 1 month

Show your work.

A) 116.54 × 12 weeks = 1398.48
1398.48 × 3% = 41.94
1398.48 + 41.94 = 1481.88

supposing if there is 4 weeks in a month

a) 466.16 × 3 = 1398.48
1398.48 × 3% = 41.95
1398.48 + 41.95 = 1440.43

b) 466.16 × 6 = 2796.96
2796.96 × 3% = 83.91
2796.96 + 83.91 = 2880.87

c) 466.16 × 12 = 5593.92
5593.92 × 3% = 167.82
5593.92 + 167.82 = 5761.74

Thought Project 9
The Speed of Light

You may have heard the expression "faster than the speed of light," but have you ever thought about how fast light travels? Although light travels very quickly, it does not move from point to point instantaneously. In other words, although it appears that light appears immediately when you flick on a lamp switch, it actually takes a small amount of time for the light rays to move from the light source to your eyes. So, you may be wondering, just how fast does light travel? Very fast! The velocity of a light ray traveling through a vacuum is 186,000 miles per second.

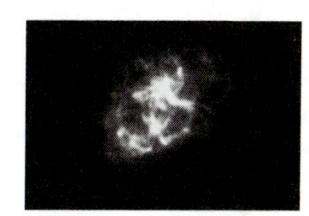

The Crab Nebula formed from the supernova documented by Chinese astronomers in 1054.
Courtesy © SPL/Photo Reserchers, Inc.

Problem:

In A.D. 1054, Chinese astronomers observed the light from a supernova in the night sky. This supernova was the incredibly powerful origin of what is now the Crab Nebula.

Using the velocity of light, devise and execute a strategy for finding when the supernova actually occurred relative to when the Chinese astronomers saw the explosion.

I. UNDERSTAND THE PROBLEM

a) Read the problem statement carefully to be sure you understand what problem you are being asked to solve. Identify the pertinent pieces of information.

- 1054 AD - the date the light has been seen
- the distance between earth & crab nebula
- How fast light travels
- what year the explosion happened

II. DEVISE A PLAN

b) What are some possible strategies for solving this problem?
- use converting strategies d = r·t
- watch the tape
- Subrat 1054AD by the distance

c) Of the strategies that were listed in b, discuss the advantages/disadvantages of each.

d = r·t would be time consuming and more difficult than just subtracting 1054AD by the distance 6,000 light years.

d) Is there any additional information that is necessary to solve the problem? If so, what? you need to know how far crab nebula is away from the earth and you also need to know what a light year is.

e) If you listed any items in d, identify some possible sources for finding this information.

you could use the internet an ecyclopedia or any other research material

Although there may be other solutions to the problem, the simplest method might be to use the algebraic relation:

Distance = Rate x Time

or, using variables:

$$d = rt$$

Notice that we have three unknown quantities in the above equation. Mathematically, this means that we can find any one of the unknown quantities if we know the other two.

III. CARRY OUT THE PLAN

f) What two quantities do we need to know in order to solve the problem?

Distance and Time

If one of the things you listed in *f* is the distance, you are correct. You will want to find the distance using one of the sources you listed in *e*.

At this point we need to pause and look again at our equation:

$$d = rt$$

g) Why is this problem slightly different from the one used in Thought Project 8?

Thought project 8 consisted of melting Ice by using energy and how much energy it would take to melt ice.

> **Math Review**
> Read: Section 2.3
> MathPro: 2.3B

h) What is required for us to complete this problem mathematically?

you need to know the rate and convert the miles per second into miles per year

52 Thought Project 9

i) Rewrite the equation in the form that is necessary to solve this problem.

186,000 miles a second — 60 seconds in a minute — 60 minutes in an hour — 24 hours in a day — 365.25 days in a year = 5,869,7136 miles a year

j) Solve the equation to determine how long before the light was witnessed by the astronomers the supernova actually occurred.

5.8697136^{12} miles a year or 4,000 years

> **Note**
> The constancy of the velocity of light is a powerful tool employed by modern day astronomers as they make measurements of the various objects in our universe.

IV. LOOK BACK

k) What are some possible sources of error in this problem solving technique?

There is no really error in this problem solving technique if you watch the video.

Thought Project 10

Continuity Equation

Problem:

Situation: A husband and wife are working in their garden one evening. While watering the grass, the wife is holding the hose horizontally and the water is flowing from the end of the hose. She twists the nozzle of the hose to partially close it and suddenly the water shoots farther from the end of the hose. This seems strange to her husband who wonders, "Why does the stream of water travel farther, since it appears that less water is flowing from the end of the hose?"

Your challenge is to give a scientific explanation for why this seemingly unnatural situation occurs.

I. UNDERSTAND THE PROBLEM

a) Reread the situation and make sure you understand what problem you are asked to solve. You may want to draw a picture to help you visualize the problem.

Skill Level I

II. DEVISE A PLAN

b) Discuss some possible problem solving strategies to solve this problem.

c) For this Thought Project, which strategy: physical experimentation, information research, or mathematics would be most likely to generate a successful solution? Why?

d) For those problems solving strategies that you eliminated, why do you think that they would not be viable problem solving options for this situation?

Math Review

It may be helpful to review section 1.2 on Variables and Equations in your Tools Book. Also see:

Read: Section 2.3

MathPro: 2.3A

III. CARRY OUT THE PLAN

Although there are a number of problem solving strategies that might be used, the most efficient approach is to use mathematics, specifically a principal called the *Continuity Equation*. This equation is written as:

$$A_1 v_1 = A_2 v_2$$

- Cross-sectional area at point 1 → A_1
- Velocity of the fluid at point 1 → v_1
- Cross-sectional area at point 2 → A_2
- Velocity of the fluid at point 2 → v_2

It may be helpful to view an illustration as in Figure 10.1.

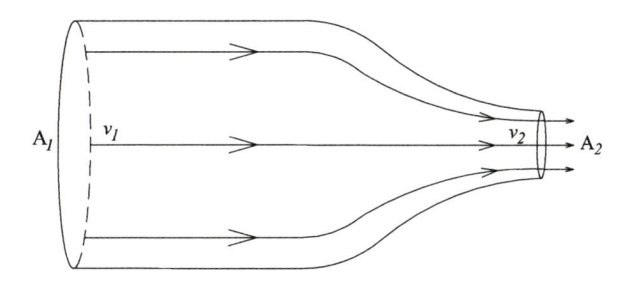

Figure 10.1

> The **cross-sectional** area of a figure is the two-dimensional surface area that is generated by slicing through the figure. In this problem, the cross-sectional areas are areas of circles.

e) Does the introduction of this equation modify your interpretation of the original problem or your strategy for solving it?

f) Choose some real numbers and show how this equation provides an answer to the husband's apparent problem. What does this equation suggest to you about the relationship between velocity and area?

g) Write out a detailed explanation of the solution to this Thought Project.

h) Suggest some other situations where the Continuity Equation could come into play.

Skill Level II

Problem:

Use the Continuity Equation to explain how jet engines provide a forward thrust for an airplane.

Skill Level III

The Continuity Equation is actually related to a powerful equation from fluid dynamics—Bernoulli's Equation.

a) Do the research necessary to find Bernoulli's Equation.

b) Identify what each of the terms in Bernoulli's Equation represents.

c) At the beginning of the Thought Project an assumption was built in to the wording of the problem that we do not need in order to use Bernoullli's Equation. What is the assumption?

d) Discuss how the Continuity Equation and Bernoulli's Equation might relate to one another.

DRAWING SKILL OPPORTUNITY 4: DRAWING PIPING

The problem we confronted in this project involved fluids entering and exiting certain cross-sectional areas.

In this Drawing Skill Opportunity, you are introduced to the standard commands that are used to develop drawings of piping in different situations.

In addition to the classroom instruction that you will receive, a listing of commands that will generate the image of a pipe is included in Appendix A.

Thought Project 11
Computer Repair Calls

Skill Level **I**

The personnel manager for a large computer company is planning to promote one of two outside computer repair technicians. Unfortunately, she has limited data on which to base the decision. The only quantitative information that is available for the last year is summarized in the following tables.

Person #1	Jan	Feb	Mar	Apr	May	Jun	Jul	Aug	Sep	Oct	Nov	Dec
No. of calls	42	65	57	39	41	55	62	38	45	52	47	61
Successful in-house repairs	29	43	38	22	28	48	50	27	30	39	31	40

(handwritten: 69, 66, 67, 56, 68, 87, 81, 71, 67, 75, 66, 66; 604, 20%, 925)

Person #2	Jan	Feb	Mar	Apr	May	Jun	Jul	Aug	Sep	Oct	Nov	Dec
No. of calls	30	25	28	32	22	21	31	29	35	33	26	32
Successful in-house repairs	18	19	22	20	15	12	19	20	30	17	20	18

(handwritten: 60, 76, 78, 63, 68, 57, 61, 69, 86, 52, 77, 56; 344, 67%, 230)

Problem:

Devise and execute a strategy that will allow the personnel manager to compare these two candidates in an objective manner.

I. DEVISE A PLAN

a) Using the above data, what are some possible ways to compare these two candidates?

you could compare both of their sucessful in house repairs monthly or yearly. Find out who has the greater percentage rate.

Thought Project 11

Math Review
Read: Section 2.7
MathPro: 2.7 B, C, D, E

II. CARRY OUT THE PLAN

b) Execute your strategy and discuss your findings.

you can compare on a monthly or yearly basis either way the first one has a higher percentage rate.

III. LOOK BACK

c) In your opinion, how valid are the summary results you derived from the data? Is there a way to increase the validity of your statistics? If so, how?

They are valid on a monthly or yearly rate you could figure it out on a quarterly basis or for a half a year ect...

d) If you were the personnel manager, what other information would you like to have before making the promotion decision for these two candidates?

*Attendence records
Attitude/personality
contributions
backround/knowledge*

e) For the information that you listed in *d*, detail a plan how you might acquire this information.

Check company records for days called off or you could have a personal interview with each person.

Thought Project 12
Designing Computer Icons

Problem:

The instructor of an introductory computer course wants to make a wall chart of the computer desktop for her students. To make it as realistic as possible, she would like the desktop icons to be proportional to the size of her 6 foot by 6 foot chart. If the icons on her 11 inch by 8 inch PC screen are 3/8 of an inch by 3/8 of an inch, how large should they be on her wall chart?

I. UNDERSTAND THE PROBLEM

a) Explain, in your own words, what the terms *desktop* and *icon* mean. If you need help, reference your computer textbook.

> Desktop — The default computer screen with software programs
>
> Icon — software programs represented by a picture on the desktop each one can be opened by double clicking on them individually.

II. DEVISE A PLAN

b) What are some of the strategies that you may use to solve this problem?

> Take the size of the P.C. and set up $8\left(\frac{3}{8}\right)$ then you'll get 5.82 and then multiply $5.82\left(\frac{3}{8}\right) = \frac{29}{8} = \underline{3"\text{ by }2.18.}$

Skill Level I

c) For those strategies that you listed in b, discuss any particular skills or materials that would be required for you to execute your strategy.

Multiply $8 \frac{3}{8} = 5.82 \left(\frac{3}{8}\right) = \frac{24}{8} =$ 3" by 2.18" then round that off to $2\frac{1}{2}$" by $2\frac{1}{2}$"

III. CARRY OUT THE PLAN

d) Execute your strategy and find the dimensions of the desktop icon on the wall chart.

*$8 \cdot 3/8 = 24/8 = 3"$
$5.8 \left(\frac{3}{8}\right) = \frac{17.46}{8} = 2.18"$
Rounded $2\frac{1}{2}$ by $2\frac{1}{2}$*

IV. LOOK BACK

e) Having used mathematics to solve the problem, is there an alternative problem solving strategy that you would suggest? Explain.

There really is no any other way to solve this problem without the use of mathematics.

f) Identify situations in which one problem solving strategy would be more advantageous than the other.

Math Review

It may be helpful to review the coverage of proportion in your Tools book:

Read: Section 2.7

MathPro: 2.7 C, D, E

Thought Project 13

Traffic Lights

Downtown Metropolis was a marvel of modern design. The streets had been laid out in a perfect grid pattern with each block measuring 500 feet in length. All of the north-south roads were called avenues while those that ran in an east-west direction were called streets. To keep traffic flowing as smoothly as possible, the city engineers timed it so that all of the traffic lights on the avenues changed to red at the same time. When the avenue lights turned red, the traffic lights on all of the streets turned green, in unison. On both the avenues and the streets, lights stayed green for 1 1/2 minutes, yellow for 30 seconds, and red for 2 minutes.

Skill Level

I

Problem:

A driver is stopped at a red light at the intersection of 5th Ave. and 6th St. He proceeds north on 6th St. to 9th Ave. where he makes a right. He then travels east for four blocks to 10th St. He takes a left on 10th St. and travels one block to his destination at the intersection of 10th St. and 10th Ave.

If, between accelerating and braking, he averages 20 miles per hour between lights, what is the shortest possible time it will take him to reach the corner of 10th and 10th?

I. UNDERSTAND THE PROBLEM

a) Draw a diagram of the problem.

b) Is this a problem with one solution or multiple solutions? Explain.

II. DEVISE A PLAN

c) What are some possible problem solving strategies for this problem?

d) Do any of the strategies that you listed in *c* have any advantages over any others?

III. CARRY OUT THE PLAN

e) Find the solution to the problem using your chosen strategy. Show your work and give your final answer.

IV. LOOK BACK

f) If you ran into difficulties solving this problem, what were they? How could they be avoided in the future?

g) To solve this problem, you used the rules of algebra. However, you were not required to write out an equation for this problem. If we choose mathematics as the problem solving tool, is a written equation always necessary? Explain.

Thought Project 14

Wiring Resistors in Series and in Parallel

In Thought Project 1 you were introduced to Ohm's Law and learned how to use it to solve the problem of a circuit with one resistor. The purpose of this Thought Project is to expand your understanding of electronics by confronting circuits that have more than one resistor.

Given a single voltage source, there are two different ways to wire two resistors into the circuit. The two possible arrangements are:

1) wiring the resistors in series
2) wiring the resistors in parallel

Series Wiring

When we say that two circuit elements (such as resistors) are wired in series, we mean that all of the electric current that passes through the first circuit element also passes through the second.

a) With the assistance of your instructor, draw the schematic of a circuit that contains a DC voltage source and two resistors wired in series.

Parallel Wiring

An alternate way to arrange the resistors is such that the electric current has a choice through which resistor it will flow. The point at which the current splits and becomes two currents is called a *junction* or a *node*.

Skill Level

I

b) Draw the schematic for this circuit with the aid of your instructor. Identify the point in the circuit at which the current divides.

Math Review

Read: Section 1.2

MathPro: 1.2 A, B, C, D

Even though these circuits have more than one resistor, Ohm's Law is still the appropriate equation to use to solve for items in the circuit. In this Thought Project, we have two resistors in the circuit, but the voltage source is only aware of the *total* resistance that the two resistors provide. In other words, Ohm's Law relates the voltage to the *total* current flow and the *total* resistance in the circuit:

$$V = IR_{Total}$$

Consequently, to use Ohm's Law, we need to find the total resistance of the two resistors wired in series as well as the total resistance of two resistors wired in parallel.

To find the total resistance of two resistors wired in series we use the equation:

$$R_{Total} = R_1 + R_2$$

To find the total resistance of two resistors wired in parallel, the equation is

$$\frac{1}{R_{Total}} = \frac{1}{R_1} + \frac{1}{R_2}$$

Problem: Two resistors in series

Situation: You and a partner have two resistors (2.2KΩ and 3.3KΩ) and a voltage source that is set to 10 Volts.

Construct the circuit with the two resistors wired in series. Measure the total current flow in the circuit and compare it to the mathematical result given by Ohm's Law.

I. UNDERSTAND THE PROBLEM

Read the problem carefully to make sure you understand exactly what you are being asked to do. It may be helpful to draw a picture of the circuit to begin.

> **Problem Solving Tips**
>
> Because the problem statement tells you to use the two different strategies of wiring the circuit and using mathematics to solve the problem, we will not itemize Step II. Devise a Plan.

II. CARRY OUT THE PLAN

Strategy 1: Mathematics

c) Using the equation for the total resistance:

$$R_{Total} = R_1 + R_2$$

find the total resistance in the circuit.

> **Math Review**
>
> To make progress on this section of the problem, we need to be able to combine two terms in a variable expression.
>
> Read: 2.1
>
> MathPro: 2.1B

d) Using Ohm's Law, with a 10 Volt source, what is the total current in the circuit?

Strategy 2: Wiring the Circuit

To begin, you will need to wire the circuit and track your measurements of current flow.

e) What is the measured value for the total current?

Trial 1:

Trial 2:

Trial 3:

Average:

f) What will be the effect on the total current if the voltage is changed up to 10.1 Volts or down to 9.9 Volts?

g) If there is a difference between your measured value and Ohm's Law, why do you think there may be a difference? Please explain the reason for this difference.

h) Does the equation for the total resistance, coupled with Ohm's Law suggest any additional measurements that might be of interest?

Wiring Resistors in Series and in Parallel

> **Problem:** Two resistors in parallel
>
> Construct the circuit with the two resistors wired in parallel. Measure the total current flow in the circuit and compare it to the mathematical result given by Ohm's Law.

Strategy 1: Mathematics

i) Using the equation for the total resistance:

$$\frac{1}{R_{Total}} = \frac{1}{R_1} + \frac{1}{R_2}$$

what would be the total resistance in the circuit?

j) Employing Ohm's Law, with a 10 Volt source, what is the total current in the circuit?

Math Review

To handle two resistors wired in parallel, you must be able to manipulate fractional expressions.

Read: Section R.2

MathPro: R.2 D

Strategy 2: Wiring the Circuit

k) What is the measured value of the total current in the circuit?

Trial 1:

Trial 2:

Trial 3:

Average:

l) If the voltage is changed up to 10.1 Volts or down to 9.9 Volts, discuss the effect on the current.

m) Explain any differences between your measured current and the predicted current from Ohm's Law.

III. LOOK BACK

n) Were the two experiments of the same difficulty? Discuss your findings.

o) In these two problems, series wiring and parallel wiring, compare the problem solving strategy method of physical experimentation with mathematics.

Skill Level II

Problem: Wire a circuit that has a 2.2 KΩ and a 3.3 KΩ resistor wired in parallel and a 4.7 KΩ resistor wired in series with this parallel combination. If the circuit has a source voltage of 10 volts, answer the following questions.

a) Draw the schematic for the circuit.

b) Measure the total current flow in the circuit. What is your reading?

c) Use mathematics to find the total resistance in the circuit.

$$R_{Total}=$$

d) Use Ohm's Law to find the total current flow in the circuit.

$$I_{Total}=$$

e) Explain any discrepancies between your measured value for the total current and the value predicted by mathematics.

Skill Level III

Problem:

Find the total current mathematically and experimentally for the following circuit (Figure 14.1):

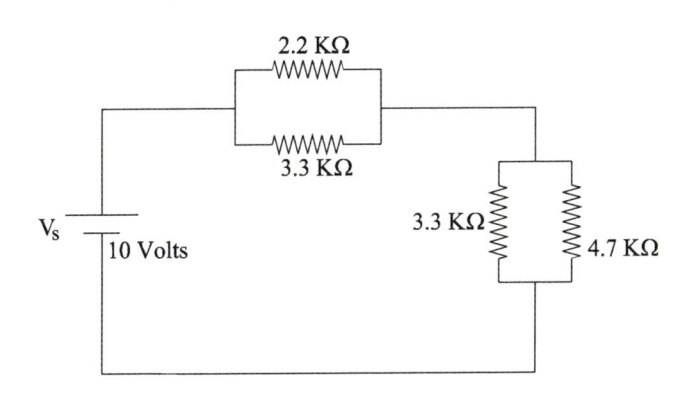

Figure 14.1

Devise and execute a strategy that will allow you to compare the measured value with the mathematically predicted value.

DRAWING SKILL OPPORTUNITY 5: DRAWING A PARALLEL CIRCUIT

In this skill opportunity, we will build on the techniques learned in the first skill opportunity and Ohm's Law. In Drawing Skill Opportunity 2, we learned how to construct the symbols and lines associated with resistors and series wiring. We have seen that to draw more complex circuits, such as a parallel or series-parallel circuits, we simply repeat the same commands.

The commands given in Appendix A as well as those given to you by your instructor are designed to teach you how to draw more complex circuits.

Thought Project 15
Genetics

One of the more controversial topics at the forefront of today's technology is the subject of cloning. This subject, once only a fantasy of science fiction, has now become a scientific reality. Although some scientists claim that cloning was inevitable once the DNA molecule was unraveled in the late 1950's by Watson and Crick, few were ready for the moral, ethical, and legal questions that arose when the sheep, Dolly, was cloned in Scotland. With the successful cloning of animals comes the question of whether or not it would be *possible* to clone a human being.

For geneticists to attack the cloning problem, a complete understanding of the biological and molecular code that makes up the human body is required. This biological code is completely "spelled out" in a very long and complicated molecule that lives within the nucleus of our cells. This molecule is the DNA molecule. DNA stands for deoxyribonucleic acid. A brief introduction to the structure of this molecule will give you an insight into the complexity of the problem that confronts those involved in this scientific endeavor.

The DNA Molecule

The complete DNA molecule is composed of two long strands that are attached together almost like the zipper on a coat. These two attached strands spiral upward in the form of a helix:

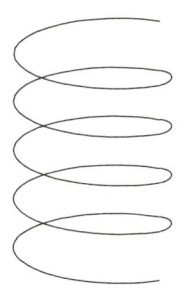

Figure 15.1 A Single Helix

Because we have two strands in this geometric form, the DNA molecule is called a *double* helix:

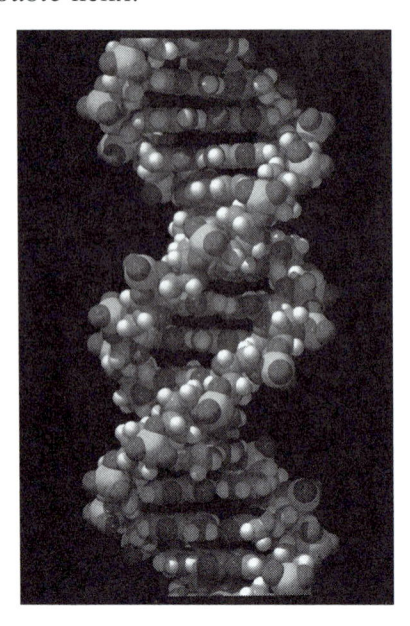

Figure 15.2 B-DNA molecule

Copyright © Ken Eward/Photo Researchers, Inc.

It is this double helix that contains the information about our eye color, hair color, and other genetic characteristics. If we go inside the molecule, we can begin to see how our genetic information is coded.

The full molecule is constructed of pieces called *nucleotides*. Each nucleotide is comprised of three pieces: a sugar molecule, a phosphate molecule, and an organic base. The sugar molecule is deoxyribose (hence the name of the molecule). This sugar molecule is bonded to the phosphate molecule. Sticking off from the side of the phosphate molecule is one of four organic bases: adenine, cytosine, guanine, or thymine.

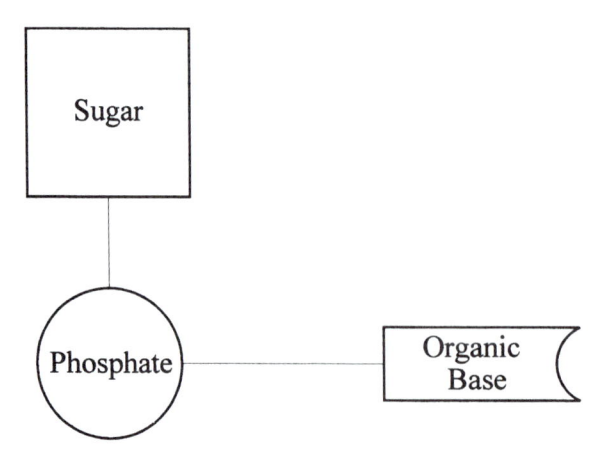

Figure 15.3 DNA nucleotide

Millions of nucleotides are joined with the sugars and phosphates to form the backbone of the strand (see Figure 15.4).

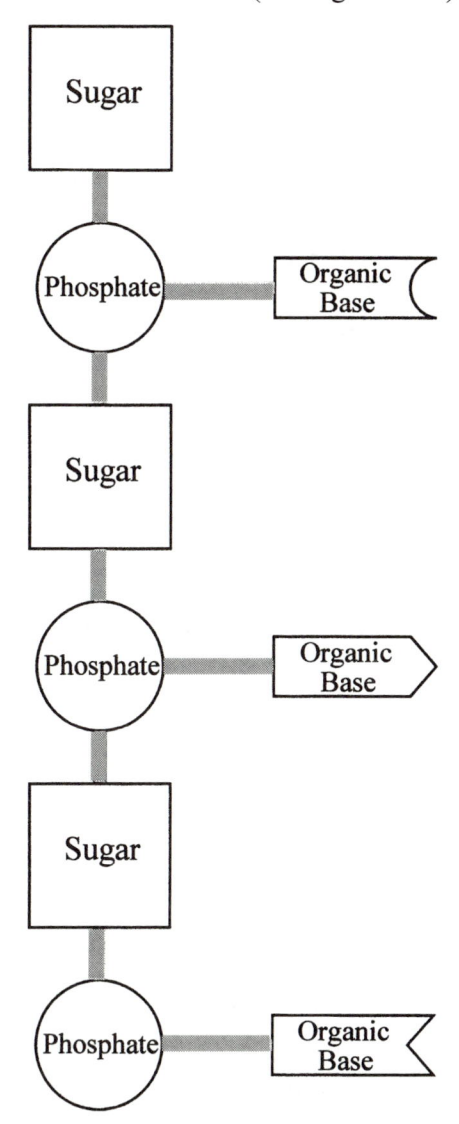

Figure 15.4 Three nucleotides in a DNA strand

Two of these strands form the double helix of the DNA by attaching themselves to one another via the organic bases. However, each of the organic bases will only bond with one other base. Adenine and thymine will bond together, as will cytosine and guanine. This means that in order for the two strands to "zip together," the appropriate bases must be across from one another (see Figure 15.5).

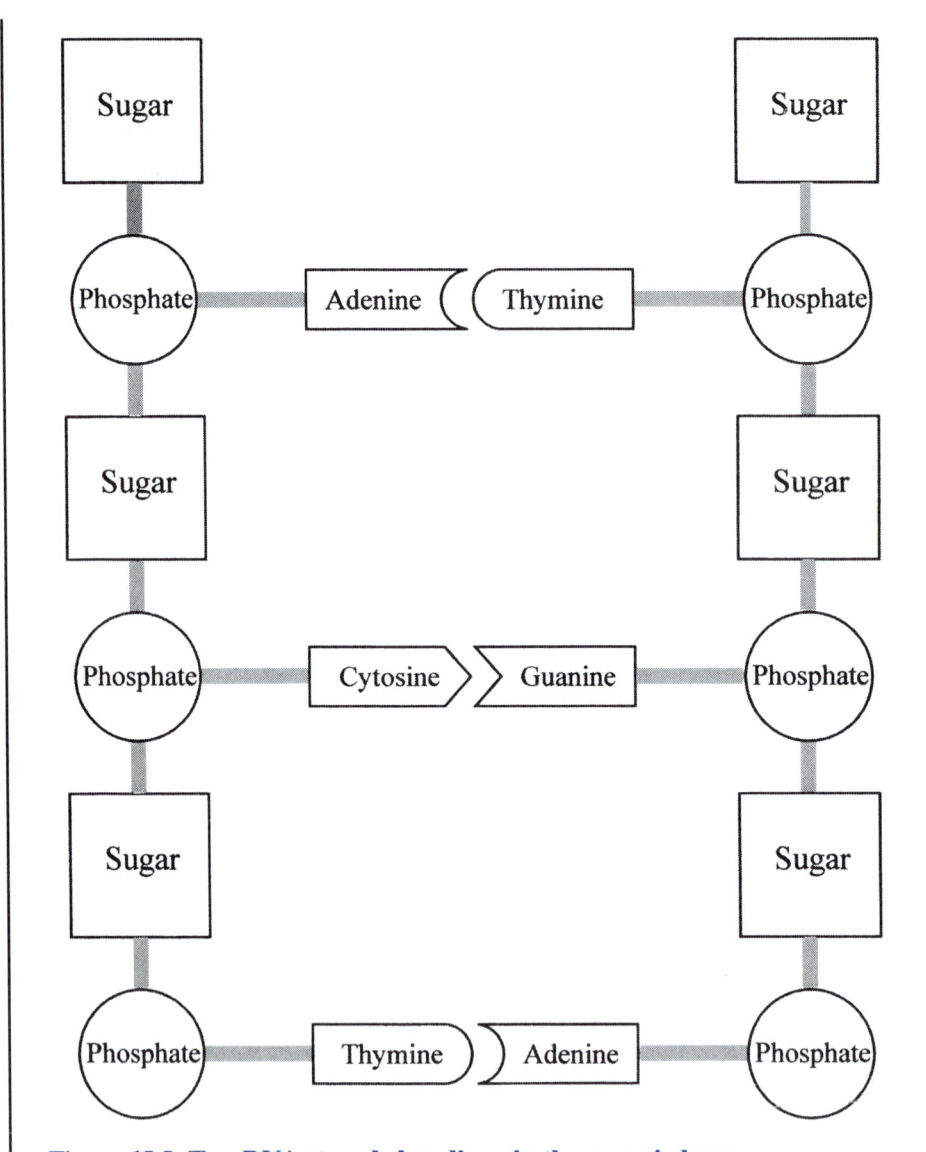

Figure 15.5 Two DNA strands bonding via the organic bases

Amazingly, an individual's genetic make-up is determined by the order in which the organic bases appear in the DNA strands. No two people have exactly the same ordering of organic bases in their DNA molecules. These strands, which are millions of nucleotides long, contain the necessary information for thousands of bodily operations. For example, when you cut your hand, your body knows exactly what type of tissue is required to repair that region. This information is contained in a certain length of the DNA strand. The information about your hair color is contained in another region of the strand. The information that comprises your individual DNA molecule came from two other DNA molecules: your mother's and your father's!

Problem:

Use the introduction to the DNA molecule as a basis for addressing the following questions.

a) How does the above discussion explain why certain diseases are genetic?

Problem Solving Tips

Practice using Pólya's four steps while working through the problems in this Thought Project.
• Make sure that you read the background information carefully and that you understand exactly what each question is asking you to do.

b) Since any one nucleotide can contain one of the four organic bases, how many different permutations of organic bases are possible for two adjacent nucleotides? Write out the possible permutations.

c) How many permutations of organic bases are possible for three adjacent organic bases? Four?

d) Using your answers from steps *b* and *c*, decide whether or not it is possible for "identical" twins to actually be identical. Explain your reasoning.

e) In your opinion, what are some of the questions that will face us as a society if we ever achieve the necessary science to clone a human being?

f) For each of the questions that you listed in *e*, what would be a strategy that would allow our society to find the answers to those questions?

Interlude II

Simplifying Radicals, Exponents, and Negative Exponents

We will take a break from problem solving to discuss alternative ways to think about and manipulate the radical expressions that we encountered in previous Thought Projects. The techniques in this Interlude will help you to make better use of the "use an equation strategy" in the forthcoming Thought Projects.

In the first two sections of this Interlude, we will discuss the methods by which we can add, subtract, multiply and/or divide two radical expressions. We will then learn how to write radical expressions in a manner that allows for even greater simplification.

Multiplying and Dividing Two Radical Expressions

When we have an expression such as

$$\sqrt{4} \cdot \sqrt{25}$$

in which we are taking the square root of both terms, we can combine them by placing them inside one radical sign. Since the expression asked for the two square roots to be multiplied, we will multiply the two terms inside the radical:

$$\sqrt{4} \cdot \sqrt{25} = \sqrt{4 \cdot 25} = \sqrt{100}$$

Let's verify this algebraic manipulation works by solving the problems separately and comparing our answer:

$$\sqrt{4} \cdot \sqrt{25} = \sqrt{100}$$
$$2 \cdot 5 = 10$$
$$10 = 10$$

This step of algebraic simplification holds true regardless of the terms that are inside the radical. Provided that the same type of root is being taken, we can always combine the two expressions under one radical symbol.

For example:

$$\sqrt[3]{5x} \cdot \sqrt[3]{4yz} = \sqrt[3]{(5x)(4yz)} = \sqrt[3]{20xyz}$$

A useful extension of this technique involves radical expressions that are divided by one another. In this case we can also combine two radical expressions into one:

$$\frac{\sqrt{100}}{\sqrt{25}} = \sqrt{\frac{100}{25}} = \sqrt{4} = 2$$

Again, let's verify that this technique yields the same numerical answer as if we had taken each step independently:

$$\frac{\sqrt{100}}{\sqrt{25}} = \sqrt{\frac{100}{25}} = \sqrt{4} = 2$$

$$\frac{10}{5} = 2$$

$$2 = 2$$

In other words, we get the same numerical result if we calculate the square roots first and then divide the results, or combine the two square roots into one. As with the technique for multiplication, the technique for division can be applied even if we are taking a root other than a square root, or if the terms inside the radicals are not numbers:

$$\frac{\sqrt[3]{x}}{\sqrt[3]{y}} = \sqrt[3]{\frac{x}{y}}$$

Adding and Subtracting Two Radical Expressions

In contrast, the rules for combining two radical expressions using addition or subtraction require that the radical expressions be identical. We must take the same type of root *and* have the same terms inside the radical. In the following examples, we can add the two expressions in *a* and *c* but cannot combine the two expressions in *b*:

a) $\sqrt{xy} + \sqrt{xy} = 2\sqrt{xy}$

b) $\sqrt{x^2 y} + \sqrt{xy}$

c) $\sqrt[3]{x} + \sqrt[3]{x} = 2\sqrt[3]{x}$

Alternative Forms of Radical Expressions

In this section of the Interlude we will discuss an alternative manner in which to express radicals; one that is particularly beneficial to the

Thought Projects in this book. Although the method is different, it follows the same rules that we learned previously.

This technique involves rewriting our radical expressions in terms of fractional exponents. The fractional exponent contains both the information that is inside the radical and the type of root that is being taken (square root, cube root, etc.).

> To write a radical expression using a fractional exponent, use the power that is on the term inside the radical as the numerator of the fraction and the root that is being taken as the denominator of the fraction.

Let's practice this technique by rewriting several different examples.

Example 1:

$$\sqrt[3]{x^2}$$

In this case, we are taking a cube root (or 3rd root) and the x inside the radical has been raised to the second power. Thus, we can rewrite the expression as:

$$\sqrt[3]{x^2} = x^{\frac{2}{3}}$$

Example 2:

$$\sqrt{x}$$

For many students working with a square root is more difficult than higher roots because, by convention, we do not include the 2 that alerts the reader that it is a "2nd" root being taken. Further, we do not include the assumed 1 that is the exponent, x^1, in this example. If we use these two pieces of assumed information, we can rewrite the expression as:

$$\sqrt{x} = x^{\frac{1}{2}}$$

Before we move on to the next example, let's briefly discuss an algebraic technique that is useful in simplifying algebraic statements.

It is possible to move terms between the numerator and the denominator of a fraction by changing the sign of the exponent on the term. For example,

$$\frac{3}{x^2}$$

can be rewritten as $3x^{-2}$.

Note that we did not change the sign on the entire term, only on the exponent.

Let's use this fact in our next example:

Example 3:

$$\frac{2}{\sqrt[4]{x^3}}$$

Expressing the denominator in terms of a fractional exponent gives us

$$\frac{2}{\sqrt[4]{x^3}} = \frac{2}{x^{\frac{3}{4}}}$$

Moving the denominator into the numerator yields

$$\frac{2}{\sqrt[4]{x^3}} = 2x^{-\frac{3}{4}}$$

We can now compare the two techniques of multiplying two radicals and expressing radicals in terms of fractional exponents and see that they actually yield the same result. We shall see that the technique of using fractional exponents allows us to combine radical expressions in the same way that we did at the beginning of this Interlude.

Suppose that we have the following radical expression:

$$\sqrt{x} \cdot \sqrt{x}$$

Because both terms have a square root we know that we can combine the two expressions:

$$\sqrt{x} \cdot \sqrt{x} = \sqrt{x \cdot x} = \sqrt{x^2} = x$$

Now, let's use fractional exponents to solve this same problem and compare our results.

Beginning with the expression, we can rewrite each radical using fractional exponents:

$$\sqrt{x} \cdot \sqrt{x} = x^{\frac{1}{2}} \cdot x^{\frac{1}{2}}$$

Because the two terms have the same base, we can combine them by adding together their exponents

$$x^{\frac{1}{2}} \cdot x^{\frac{1}{2}} = x^{\frac{1}{2} + \frac{1}{2}} = x^1 = x$$

In both cases, we arrived at a final answer of x.

It is advantageous to know as many mathematical tools as possible to become effective problem solvers. The techniques discussed in this Interlude are only a few of the many mathematical tools that are available to help us in problem solving.

Math Review

For more detailed explanations and exercises

Read: Section 9.1–9.4

MathPro: 9.2 A, B, C

9.3 A, B

9.4 B

Thought Project 16
Number Puzzle

In this Thought Project, we take a break from real world applications to attack an abstract thought problem. An abstract problem, like this one, does not lend itself to many of the visual, physical, or research techniques that have been employed thus far. However, it is still solvable if approached with an appropriate strategy.

Example: The numbers two and four share an interesting relationship. Did you know that 2 raised to the 4th power is the same as 4 raised to the 2nd power because both are equal to 16?

In equation form:

$$2^4 = 4^2$$
$$16 = 16$$

On the left side of the equation, 2 is the base and 4 is the exponent. On the right side, 4 is the base and 2 is the exponent.

This relationship between the bases and exponents is definitely not the norm. For example, it is certainly not true that 3 to the 7th is equal to 7 to the 3rd power:

$$3^7 \neq 7^3$$

Skill Level I

Math Review
For a review of exponents see your Tool Book.
Read: 4.1
MathPro: 4.1A

Problem:

Find two other unequal numbers that share the same relationship as 2 and 4.

I. UNDERSTAND THE PROBLEM
Make sure that you fully understand the problem that you are being asked to solve.

II. DEVISE A PLAN

a) What are some possible problem solving strategies for this problem?

b) Of the strategies that you listed in *a*, do any of them have constraints that make them more difficult than the rest?

c) What problem solving strategy will you use to solve this problem?

III. CARRY OUT THE PLAN

d) What are two numbers that provide a solution to the problem?

IV. LOOK BACK

e) If you were able to access any tool that you desired, how might you solve the problem differently?

Thought Project 17

Planning for a Nuclear Blast

From the moment the first atomic bomb exploded over Hiroshima, Japan, in August 1945, every man, woman, and child has lived with the threat of nuclear war. Although, the dissolution of the Soviet Union and the end of the Cold War has lessened this threat, most Americans would argue that the possibility still exists. As we go about our daily lives, we trust that government officials are taking the necessary steps to protect us from nuclear war.

Skill Level I

Problem:

You and a partner are appointed to the President's cabinet as the national nuclear advising team. Your job is to provide the President with recommendations for nuclear safety and citizen response in the event of a nuclear assault.

I. UNDERSTAND THE PROBLEM

a) Is it possible to break this problem into smaller problems? If so, list some of the smaller problems.

An example of the tremendous power of a nuclear blast.

Copyright © Hulton Eetty

b) Are there different problem solving strategies for each smaller problem? Explain.

II. DEVISE A PLAN

c) Draft a strategy for how you and your partner are going to divide the problem.

d) What are some of the possible resources available to you to help you gather the information for the President?

III. CARRY OUT THE PLAN

While doing research, you probably realized that a complete recommendation to the President must include an evacuation plan to be followed in the event of a nuclear strike. But how will you go about constructing that plan? First you will need to determine how far the radiation from a nuclear blast is likely to spread. Physics tells us that the spread of the radiation is directly proportional to the energy produced by the blast. Consequently, you must know how much energy is produced by the nuclear blast.

To find that critical piece of information, you must use the equation that is at the heart of all nuclear reactions, namely Einstein's famous:

$$E = mc^2$$

where E is Energy, m is Mass, c is Speed of light, and the 2 indicates Square.

which states that mass and energy are two different forms of the same physical quantity. In a nuclear explosion, some of the mass that is inside the nucleus of the atom is turned into energy. By translating Einstein's mathematical sentence into words, we see that:

"The equivalent energy (E) of a mass (m) can be found by multiplying the mass by the speed of light squared."

e) Does this discussion modify your initial strategy or research? If so, how?

IV. LOOK BACK

f) In addition to Einstein's equation, are there any other crucial facts that you need to prepare a complete briefing for the President?

Math Review

Consult your Tools for Problem Solving text for an introduction to bases and exponents.

Read: Section 4.1

MathPro: 4.1A

Albert Einstein (1879–1955) Nobel prize winning German physicist who invented the theory of relativity, and discovered the photoelectric effect.

Copyright © Associated Press

Skill Level II

Problem:

Given that the speed of light is 3×10^8 m/s, calculate the equivalent amount of energy available in 1 Kg of material.

Notice that in the problem statement, we do not identify whether the material referenced is dynamite, nitroglycerin, lead, etc. Give a reasonable physical explanation as to why knowledge of the type of material is not needed to calculate the energy.

Skill Level III

Problem:

Execute the necessary research to find the amount of energy liberated in the explosion over Hiroshima, Japan. Find the amount of mass that is equivalent to this amount of energy.

DRAWING SKILL OPPORTUNITY 6: THE EXPLODE COMMAND

This Thought Project lends itself to introducing the EXPLODE command included in the software. This command's function fits well with the subject of this Thought Project since its purpose is to take a solid figure and break it into its constituent surfaces. The EXPLODE command can be used to break down these surfaces into smaller parts such as lines, arcs, and points.

Thought Project 18
The Power Rule

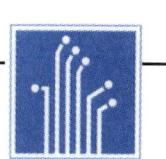

In Thought Project 1 we introduced the concepts of voltage, current, and resistance. These three principles are important ideas as we move into our next exploration and warrant a quick review:

Voltage is the quantity that causes the electrical current to flow. It can be thought of as the electrical pressure in the circuit and is measured in units of Volts.

Current is a measurement of the rate at which the electricity flows through the circuit. It is analogous to the current flowing in a stream and is measured in units of Amps.

Resistance measures how much opposition the electric current encounters as it flows through a type of material or device. Resistance is measured in Ohms.

In this Thought Project you will explore the concept of resistance by analyzing the physical result of this current opposition.

Heat and Energy

James Joule was one of the first people to do experiments illustrating that heat and energy are the same thing. In other words, if you add heat to a physical system, you have added energy to the system. Conversely, if you subtract heat from a system, you have subtracted energy from the system. This interplay between heat and energy has a direct impact on our discussion of resistors.

Although there are other factors involved, the main source of resistance is the friction caused inside the resistor. As anyone who has ever slid down a gym rope too quickly can tell you, *friction produces heat*! Inside the circuit, we know that as the current flows through the resistor, heat is generated by the friction. This heat is dissipated into the air, etc., surrounding the resistor.

Power

Because the resistor is giving off heat, it is giving off energy. Consequently, the circuit is losing energy because of the heat lost by the resistor. In electronics our focus is not so much on the heat or energy lost by the resistor, but on the *power* that is lost across the resistor by these events.

Skill Level I

James Prescott Joule (1818–1889) British physicist who established experimentally that heat is a form of energy.

Courtesy of the Library of Congress

Power, measured in Watts, is the rate at which the energy of a system is changing and is defined as:

$$\text{Power} = \frac{\text{the change in the energy}}{\text{the change in the time}}$$

The power dissipated by the resistor is found using:

$$P = I^2 R$$

where P is Power, I is Current, R is Resistance, and the ^{2} indicates Square.

Problem:

Find the power dissipated by an 8.2KΩ resistor if it is connected to a 10 Volt source. To solve this problem you are to devise, construct, and execute *two different* experiments that will find the power dissipated by a resistor.

Math Review

Read: Section 4.1A
MathPro: 4.1A

I. UNDERSTAND THE PROBLEM

Read the problem statement carefully and make sure that you understand what you are being asked to do. Review any terms or ideas that are unclear to you by rereading the background information or referring back to previous Thought Projects.

II. DEVISE A PLAN

a) Explain your two problem solving strategies.

Hint

Look at Ohm's Law in Thought Project 1.

b) Do both of your strategies require the same equipment? What equipment does each require?

III. CARRY OUT THE PLAN

c) What is the power dissipated using your first strategy?

d) What is the power dissipated using your second strategy?

e) If your two results differ, what are possible explanations for the differences?

f) Does the fact that I has been raised to the 2nd power affect the error in any way?

g) Is there a way to use mathematics to predict or confirm your experimental results? If so, explain it.

IV. LOOK BACK

h) Of these two problem solving options, experimentation and mathematics, are both equally viable? Explain.

i) If either, or both, of your experimental results do not agree with the mathematical result, what possible reasons might explain this difference?

Thought Project 19

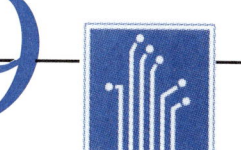

Deriving the Power Wheel

By combining the power equation, P=I²R, from Thought Project 18 with Ohm's Law, V=IR, we can find many useful equations. These equations can be visually summarized in the chart normally referred to as the Power Wheel. This chart includes the basic equations and relationships that are involved in early direct current electronics theory. This chart usually takes a form similar to:

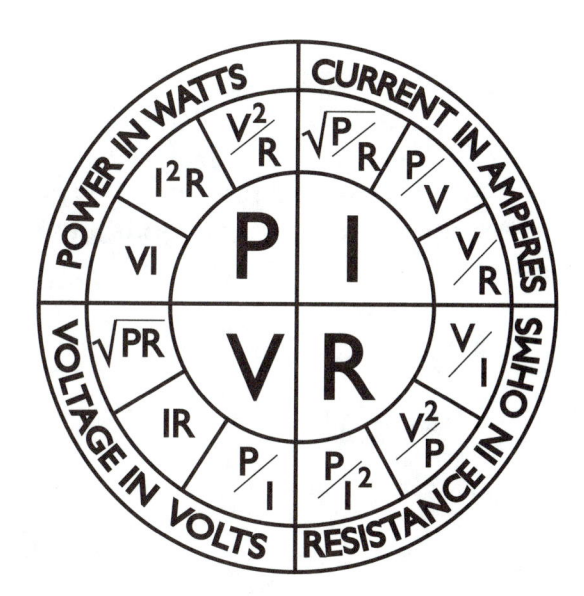

Figure 19.1 Power Wheel

The equations that this table summarizes are:

Power:
$$P = IV$$
$$P = I^2 R$$
$$P = \frac{V^2}{R}$$

Skill Level

I

Current:
$$I = \sqrt{\frac{P}{R}}$$
$$I = \frac{P}{V}$$
$$I = \frac{V}{R}$$

Resistance:
$$R = \frac{V}{I}$$
$$R = \frac{V^2}{P}$$
$$R = \frac{P}{I^2}$$

Voltage:
$$V = \sqrt{PR}$$
$$V = IR$$
$$V = \frac{P}{I}$$

Problem:

Believe it or not, all of the equations that are listed in the Power Wheel can actually be found by taking the two equations:

$$P = I^2 R$$

$$V = IR$$

and manipulating them using the rules of algebra.

Using only the two equations listed above, derive all of the equations in the Power Wheel.

I. UNDERSTAND THE PROBLEM

a) What is the advantage of being able to perform algebraic manipulations of this type?

b) Are there other situations in which these types of problem solving skills would be beneficial? If so, identify some of them.

II. DEVISE A PLAN

c) Identify the algebraic skills you need to solve the problem.

III. CARRY OUT THE PLAN

d) Execute the algebraic manipulations that are required to produce all of the equations in the Power Wheel. Show your work.

> **Math Review**
>
> To complete this exercise, you need to understand the relationship between exponents and roots, and you need to manipulate algebraic expressions.
>
> Read: Section 9.1
>
> MathPro: 9.1

IV. LOOK BACK

e) There are two different problem solving strategies that can be used to address the Power Wheel. We have already discussed how to derive the equations. The other method is to memorize all of the equations that are shown on the wheel. Discuss and contrast the merits of these two problem solving strategies as they relate to the Power Wheel and to other situations.

DRAWING SKILL OPPORTUNITY 7: DRAWING A CIRCLE INSIDE A CIRCLE

In this Thought Project we learned new problem solving skills for constructing a table that will aid you in further electronic studies. In this Drawing Skill Opportunity, we will learn the commands required to generate a clean, geometrically precise Power Wheel.

This skill opportunity draws on the previously learned skill of creating circular figures. It also introduces a new skill of inserting text into a drawing. On many ocassions in your technical career you will be required to attach additional text to the drawings that you create. This skill opportunity provides a springboard to learn this important concept.

One set of commands that will generate the Power Wheel are in Appendix A.

Thought Project

Baseballs and the Moon

Our goal in this Thought Project is to marry together several of the problem solving techniques that we have discussed previously. In most real world situations, more than one problem solving strategy is required to find a worthwhile solution. In order to solve this problem, we will be required to incorporate several different techniques.

Skill Level I

Problem:

Would one mole of baseballs fit into earth's moon?

I. UNDERSTAND THE PROBLEM

a) What are the key pieces of information in this problem? Are there any terms that you do not recognize? Explain.

Hint

If one of the terms that you do not recognize is *mole*, try researching the work done by Amadeo Avogadro.

Thought Project 20

Amadeo Avogadro
(1776–1856) Italian physicist who studied the properties of gases.

Copyright © SPL/Photo Researchers

Math Review

It may be helpful to review the Appendix on Geometry in the Tools book.

Read: Section A.5

Hint

The meaning of the term *mole* has changed during the last fifty years. Historically its definition involved molecular weights. However, in modern usage, a mole is assumed to be equivalent to Avogadro's Number, 6.02×10^{23}.

Thus, if we have a mole of some object, we have 6.02×10^{23} of that object.

II. DEVISE A PLAN

b) Discuss possible strategies that you can use to solve this problem. Can you identify more than one useful strategy?

c) Does the strategy that you listed in *b*, require using only mathematics, physical measurements, or do you need to use both? Explain.

d) Is there any important information or data missing that is needed to solve the problem?

e) List the steps that are required to solve this problem effectively.

III. CARRY OUT THE PLAN

f) Execute your strategy and solve the problem. Summarize your results below.

IV. LOOK BACK

g) Was the strategy that you employed the most efficient method of solving the problem? If you were to work the problem again would you do anything differently? Explain.

Skill Level II

Problem:

Using your own calculator, devise and execute a strategy to determine how many of these calculators would fit in your current classroom. (Assume no furniture or people are in the room.)

Skill Level III

Problem:

Devise and execute a strategy for determining the number of identical copies of the continental United States that would fit on the surface of the earth.

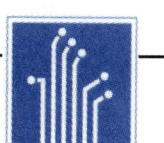

Thought Project 21
Working with Electric Current

In Thought Project 1, we discussed the concept of an electric current. We defined it simply as the amount of electricity that flows past a point in the circuit. In this Thought Project, we will analyze the current in slightly more detail.

Electric Current

Electric current is actually caused by the motion of *electric charges* inside a circuit. The electric charges are carried by the electrons inside the circuit. The magnitude of the electric current is determined by the number of electrons that move past a point in the circuit. For example, a large electric current means that we have a large number of electrons moving past a given point in the circuit. The amount of electric charge carried by each electron (measured in Coulombs) is:

.00000000000000000160217733 C

This number can be written more conveniently using *scientific notation* as $1.60217733 \times 10^{-19}$ C. Because each electron carries an extremely small amount of charge, it takes a large quantity of electrons to produce a viable current.

Given this background information on electric current, we are prepared to take a closer look at Amperes, which are the units in which current is measured.

> For a current of 1 Ampere to flow through a circuit, a total of 1 Coulomb of charge must pass by every second.

In equation form, Amperes are defined as:

$$1\,Amp = \frac{1C}{1\sec}$$

Math Review
Read: Section 4.2C
MathPro: 4.2C

Thought Project 21

Problem:

Find the number of electrons that must pass by a given point in a circuit each second to produce 10 Amps of current flow.

Solve the problem and explain your answer.

Problem Solving Tips

1. Make sure you understand what the problem is asking you to do.
2. You have been given the formula to use in solving the equation. Make sure you know how to use it.
3. Does your answer make sense? Does it satisfy the question asked?

Thought Project 22

The Mass of the Earth

Some philosophers and scientists in our society claim that the same technology that appears to be advancing our culture is actually reducing our creativity. They think that our growing dependence on technology is causing us to lose some of our abstract problem solving abilities. In this Thought Project you will have the opportunity to demonstrate your abilities to solve abstract problems without relying on modern technology.

Use your imagination to transport yourself back to an earlier day when scientists and astronomers used only simple instruments, but great minds, to tackle some of the big ideas of their day. Consider, for example, the work of Johannes Kepler and Isaac Newton in the 17th and 18th centuries. These gentlemen performed calculations and experiments that first showed the mass of our planet.

The mass of an object, simply put, is a measurement of the amount of "stuff" in the object. The larger the mass of the object, the more "stuff" it contains. Both Kepler and Newton played major roles in finding that the mass of the earth is:

5,980,000,000,000,000,000,000,000 Kg

Working with this very large number is difficult. Fortunately, we can express large numbers in a much simpler way using *scientific notation*. This technique uses the fact that every place in a number corresponds to a different factor of 10. For example, in the number 524, the 2 is in the tens place (10^1) and the 5 is in the hundreds place (10^2). To express the mass of the earth in scientific notation we move the decimal point (currently on the far right side of our number) to the left. For every space that we move it, we acquire another factor of 10. It is conventional to stop when we are left with a single digit to the left of the decimal point.

Since we need to move the decimal places 24 spaces to the left, the number can be expressed as:

5.98×10^{24} Kg

Skill Level

I

A view of the earth taken from space.

Copyright © Chris Bjornberg/Photo Researchers

Math Review

Read: Section 4.2C
MathPro: 4.2C

Problem:

You and your team know the answer to the question "What is the mass of the earth?" Your challenge in this Thought Project is to devise a strategy for finding the mass of the earth using only the equations and equipment that were available to scientists in the late 17th and early 18th centuries.

Sir Isaac Newton (1642–1727) English mathematician/scientist whose contributions include calculus, and theories of gravity, mechanics, and optics.

Courtesy of the Library of Congress

I. UNDERSTAND THE PROBLEM

a) Think about your need to solve this problem using only 17th–18th century tools and methodologies. List and discuss some of these constraints.

b) What information is necessary for you to solve this problem given these constraints?

II. DEVISE A PLAN

c) List some possible strategies for finding the mass of the earth.

d) Does your team favor a physical experiment or mathematics to address this problem? Explain.

e) If you favor an experiment, discuss the equipment involved and the data you will attempt to collect. If, however, you think mathematics is the more efficient approach, what is your starting point?

If you researched the work of Newton and Kepler, you found two key equations to help in solving the problem. Newton's *Law of Universal Gravitation* is used to measure the gravitational force between two masses. This equation states:

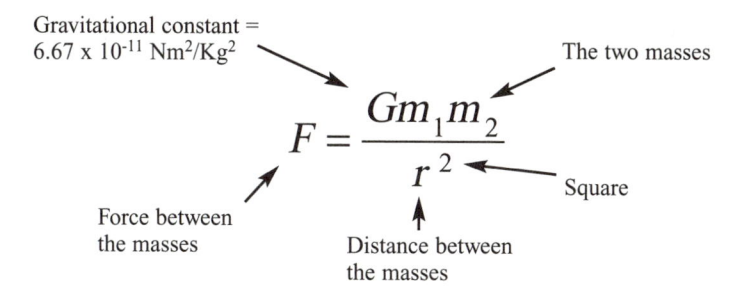

$$F = \frac{Gm_1 m_2}{r^2}$$

- Gravitational constant = 6.67×10^{-11} Nm²/Kg²
- The two masses
- Square
- Force between the masses
- Distance between the masses

Johannes Kepler (1571–1630) German astronomer who formulated three laws of planetary motion.

A picture of Newton's Law may be clearer.

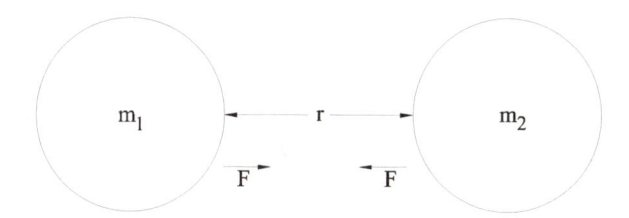

Figure 22.1 Newton's Law of Gravitation

Kepler's *Law of Periods* (see Figure 22.2) relates how long it takes a satellite (such as a moon or a planet) to orbit a central mass to the distance that the satellite is away from the central mass:

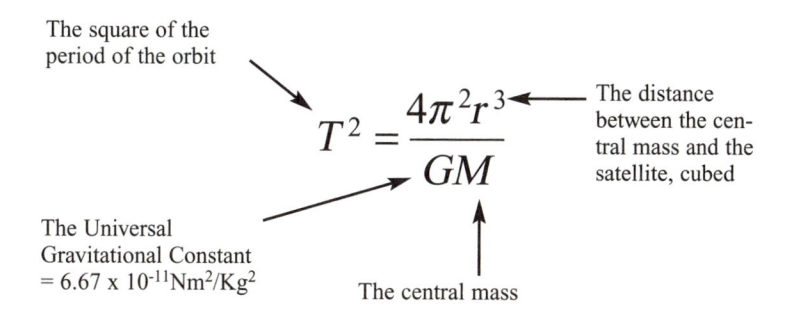

$$T^2 = \frac{4\pi^2 r^3}{GM}$$

- The square of the period of the orbit
- The distance between the central mass and the satellite, cubed
- The Universal Gravitational Constant = 6.67×10^{-11} Nm²/Kg²
- The central mass

Math Review

It may be helpful to review the section on variables and equations in your Tools book.
Read: Section 1.2
MathPro: Section 1.2B

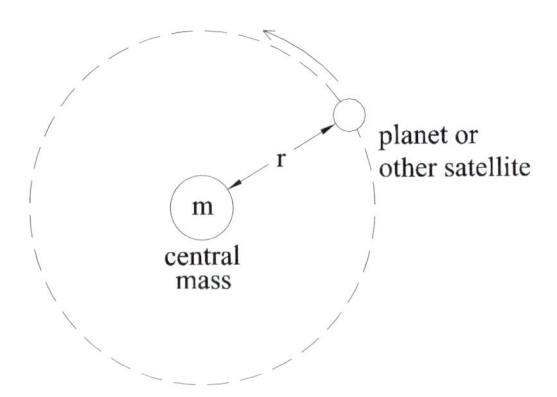

Figure 22.2 Kepler's Law of Periods

f) Does the knowledge of these formulas make you think that you should change your original problem solving strategy? Why or why not?

III. CARRY OUT THE PLAN

g) Execute your strategy and calculate the mass of the earth.

h) Did your value differ from the known value? What might be some reasons for this difference?

IV. LOOK BACK

i) Discuss how the problem solving strategy you employed would be different had you had the resources of the 21st century at your disposal.

j) Does the 300 year difference in time impact the two strategies of physical experiment and mathematics equally? Explain.

Skill Level II

Problem:

Given that the distance from the earth to the sun is 1.5×10^{11} m, and that the mass of the sun is 1.9×10^{30} Kg, use Kepler's Law of Periods to find the period of the earth's orbit.

a) Show how to express your answer in years.

Thought Project 22

b) If your answer does not agree with the accepted earth orbit period of 365.25 days, explain the discrepancy.

Skill Level III

According to Newton's Law of Gravitation, all objects with mass attract one another. This law implies that all of the atoms that make up a star, such as our sun, are gravitationally attracted to one another. If so, how is it that the sun is able to resist all of this internal attraction between its atoms and not collapse in upon itself?

Problem:

Devise and execute a problem solving strategy that will yield a reasonable *physical* explanation for how a star is able to resist collapsing under its own gravitational attraction.

Interlude III

Polynomials

When solving technical problems, you will encounter equations with expressions that have more than one term. For example,

$$4x^3+5x^2-7x+2$$

This type of expression is called a *polynomial* (remember that the prefix *poly* means many) and is the subject of this Interlude.

The first step in solving polynomial expressions is to simplify them. There are many different approaches to simplifying polynomials including addition, subtraction, multiplication, division, or even raising them to a power.

Adding and Subtracting Polynomial Expressions

For two terms in a polynomial to be combined using addition or subtraction, they must have the same *base* and the same *exponent*.

$$\text{Base} \rightarrow x^2 \leftarrow \text{Exponent}$$

For example, let's add the following two polynomials:

$$(2x^3+4x+3)+(5x^3+6x^2+x+7)$$

In this case, removing the parentheses does not alter the signs on any of the terms:

$$2x^3+4x+3+5x^3+6x^2+x+7$$

Now we are ready to combine "like terms" (terms that have the same base and the same exponent).

First, let's combine the terms that have been raised to the 3rd power:

$$2x^3+5x^3=7x^3$$

Math Review
Read: Section 4.1
MathPro: 4.1B

Math Review
A more in-depth treatment of the topics in this Interlude are found in your math Tools book.
Read: Sections 4.3, 4.4, 4.5
MathPro: 4.3 D, E
4.4 A, B
4.5 C, D

Next, we'll combine the terms that are raised to the first power:

$$4x + x = 5x$$

Notice that we interpret "x" as having a coefficient of 1 on the second term, thus yielding 5 in the addition.

Adding together our constant terms:

$$3 + 7 = 10$$

Lastly, note that we only have one term that has been raised to the 2nd power and that it cannot be coupled with any other terms.

Thus,

$$(2x^3 + 4x + 3) + (5x^3 + 6x^2 + x + 7) = 7x^3 + 6x^2 + 5x + 10$$

(Although the answer would not be wrong if the terms were put into a different order, it is conventional to express the answer in order of decreasing exponents.)

Multiplying Polynomials

Multiplication of polynomials is based on the distributive property. Each of the terms in the first polynomial must be multiplied by each of the terms in the second polynomial. This means, for example, that if we have three terms in the first polynomial and three terms in the second polynomial, we will have nine multiplications to execute.

As an example, let's carry out the following polynomial multiplication:

$$(2x^2 + 5x)(4x^3 + 5x^2 + 3)$$

Notice that to carry out this multiplication, we must be able to handle expressions such as $x^2 x^3$.

> If two variable terms are multiplied together, *and have the same base*, add the exponents.

Thus,

$$x^2 x^3 = x^{2+3} = x^5$$

Turning back to the example, we see that the $2x^3$ must be multiplied by each of the three terms in the second polynomial, as does the $5x$.

First we do the multiplication:

$$(2x^2 + 5x)(4x^3 + 5x^2 + 3)$$
$$= 8x^5 + 10x^4 + 6x^2 + 20x^4 + 25x^3 + 15x$$

Notice that the numerical coefficients that were in front of each term were also multiplied together, i.e. (2 × 4 = 8)

Math Review

Read: Section 4.6
MathPro: 4.6 A

Math Review

Read: Section 4.1
MathPro: 4.1B

Adding together those terms that have the same base and the same exponent, and expressing the answer in descending order gives us the polynomial expressed in its simplest form:

$$(2x^2+5x)(4x^3+5x^2+3) = 8x^5+30x^4+25x^3+6x^2+15x$$

Raising a Polynomial to a Power

Having discussed how to multiply two polynomials, we may now review how to raise a polynomial to a power. Remember that an exponent on an expression tells us how many times we are to multiply that expression by itself. This means that if we have a polynomial expression of the form:

$$(3x^2-4x)^2$$

we are to take $(3x^2 - 4x)$ and multiply it by itself.

$$(3x^2-4x)^2 = (3x^2-4x)(3x^2-4x)$$
$$(3x^2-4x)^2 = 9x^4-12x^3-12x^3+16x^2$$
$$(3x^2-4x)^2 = 9x^4-24x^3+16x$$

Applications

Ohm's Law Revisited This technique used in simplifying polynomials is useful in the real world because it allows us to reduce the complexity of problems. For example, in Thought Project 1, we were introduced to Ohm's Law which relates the current flow through a resistor, the value of the resistance, and the voltage source driving the current flow using:

$$V = IR$$

If the current and the resistance are time dependent, we can still use Ohm's Law. To arrive at a time-dependent expression for the voltage, we simply carry out the polynomial multiplication required when multiplying I and R.

Example

Suppose that the current through a resistor is given by I = (2t + 3) and that the resistance is given by R = ($3t^2$ + 4t). Find an expression for the voltage drop across the resistor.

Solution

We can find an expression for the voltage by using Ohm's Law and multiplying together the current and the resistance:

$$V = IR$$
$$V = (2t+3)(3t^2+4t)$$
$$V = 6t^3+8t^2+9t^2+12t$$
$$V = 6t^3+17t^2+12t$$

> **Math Review**
>
> Consult the Geometry Appendix in your Tools book for more information about area.
>
> Read: Section A.4

Working with Rectangles Another practical example is taken from our work with geometric figures. Suppose the width of a certain rectangle is expressed as $x^2 + 4x$, and the length of the rectangle is $5x + 7$. To find the area of the rectangle (the length times the width) we must use polynomial multiplication.

[rectangle with $5x + 7$ on the side and $x^2 + 4x$ on the bottom]

Solution

$$\text{Area} = (5x+7)(x^2+4x)$$
$$\text{Area} = 5x^3 + 20x^2 + 7x^2 + 28x$$
$$\text{Area} = 5x^3 + 27x^2 + 28x$$

Thought Project 23
Projectile Motion A

Skill Level I

In the physical sciences we must often distinguish between those equations and relationships that can be derived mathematically versus those that are purely *empirical*. By empirical we mean that the terms in the equation are included because they predict what we see in an experiment. Through trial and error, we have found the equation that will work. There is no profound mathematical basis for the equation.

An example of an empirical equation is the *displacement equation* from Newtonian physics:

$$y = v_0 t + \frac{1}{2} a t^2$$

This rather formidable equation is used to predict the motion of projectiles. Before we move on, lets examine each term in the equation:

y is the total vertical displacement of the object. In this Thought Project, we will use meters to measure how far an object moves or the *displacement* of the object.

v_0 is the initial velocity of the object. This velocity, measured in meters per second (m/s), is how fast the object is moving at the beginning of the problem.

t is the time that corresponds to the displacement. If we know where the object is located, it is possible to solve for when the object is at this location. Conversely, if we know the time of interest, we can insert it and find the displacement.

a is the acceleration on the object. Accelerations change the velocities of objects. If the acceleration is in the same direction as the velocity of the object, the object will move faster. If the acceleration is applied in the opposite direction of the object's velocity, the object will slow down. When dealing with vertical problems, we normally must consider the acceleration caused by gravity. Gravitational acceleration is directed straight downward on the object and is given by 9.8 m/s^2.

120 Thought Project 23

Problem:

Devise and execute an experiment that will yield the time that it takes a marble to drop from a table to the floor. Compare your experimental result with that predicted by the displacement equation.

I. UNDERSTAND THE PROBLEM

a) Read the problem statement carefully. How many steps are required to solve this problem?

Step I: Performing an Experiment

II. DEVISE A PLAN

b) Write down the steps in your experimental procedure and identify the equipment that is necessary to carry it out.

c) Do you see any potential problems with your methodology?

III. CARRY OUT THE PLAN

d) Conduct five trials of your proposed experiment. Record your results and their average in the table below.

	Time to hit the floor
Trial 1	
Trial 2	
Trial 3	
Trial 4	
Trial 5	
Average	

IV. LOOK BACK

e) How successful was your experiment? Would you modify it in any way? Explain.

Step 2: Using the Displacement Equation

III. CARRY OUT THE PLAN

f) Using your own words, explain what each of the terms in the displacement equation represents.

Problem Solving Tips

You have been given the strategy of using the displacement equation. The critical steps are to carry out the plan and look back to understand what you have learned.

Math Review

Read: Section 10.2

MathPro: 10.2 A

g) If the object is dropped (as opposed to thrown) straight downward, what is the initial velocity of the object?

h) What will be the total distance traveled by the marble?

i) If you incorporate the information from g and h, what form does the displacement equation take?

j) Execute the algebra necessary to solve for the time that it would take for the marble to hit the ground.

IV. LOOK BACK

k) In the process of solving your equation, you should have found two solutions. Are both solutions reasonable physically? Explain.

l) If your experimental result did not agree with your mathematical result, discuss possible reasons for this discrepancy.

Skill Level

II

Problem:

In the displacement equation we do not give the mass of the marble that is being used. In your opinion, when does the mass of an object and/or the size of an object affect the time that it takes to hit the floor? Explain your reasoning.

Hint

Hint: Think about the ways (if any) that the experimental results would have been effected had it had been done on the moon.

Thought Project 23

Skill Level III

When an object falls in the earth's atmosphere its velocity cannot increase indefinitely. As the velocity of the object increases a quantity called the *drag* also increases. Eventually, a balance between the two is achieved and the object reaches its *terminal velocity*. This terminal velocity is the maximum speed that an object will achieve during its freefall.

Problem:

Execute the necessary research to find an equation that will enable you to calculate the terminal velocity of a freely-falling object.

a) Identify what each of the terms in the equation represents.

b) Insert some real-world numbers and find an approximate value for the terminal velocity of an object of your choice.

Thought Project 24

Projectile Motion B

As a continuation of Thought Project 23, let's see what happens if we reverse the direction of the marble's motion. As we will observe, this simple reversal of direction adds complexity to the problem.

Skill Level I

Problem 1:

Situation: A marble is shot straight upward with an initial velocity of 6 m/s. Design an experiment that will allow you to measure how long it takes for the marble to reach a height of 1 meter.

I. UNDERSTAND THE PROBLEM

Review the problem statement to make sure that you understand the question that you are being asked to solve.

II. DEVISE A PLAN

a) Explain, as completely as possible, the structure of your experiment. If possible, make a sketch of your experimental setup.

b) What equipment would you need to conduct your experiment?

c) Do you think that your experiment will yield an exact result? Why or why not?

III. LOOK BACK

d) After thinking through your proposed experiment, would you suggest a physical experiment as the appropriate problem solving strategy for this situation? Why or why not?

Problem Solving Tips

Note that in this project you are not actually required to execute your experiment. Thus, we will skip Step III Carry Out the Plan.

Problem 2:

Use the displacement equation from Thought Project 23 to find the time when the marble will reach a height of 1 meter from its initial position.

I. UNDERSTAND THE PROBLEM

e) In the previous Thought Project, the displacement of the marble, the velocity of the marble, and the acceleration on the marble were all in the same direction (downward). Is that the case in this Thought Project? Explain.

f) Based on the information you are given, what form would the displacement equation take?

II. DEVISE A PLAN

g) Can this equation be solved using the same algebraic rules as the equation in the previous Thought Project? If not, what makes this equation different?

Math Review

Read: Section 10.2
MathPro: 10.2A

III. CARRY OUT THE PLAN

h) Execute the necessary algebra to find the time when the marble will be located 1m above ground. Show your work.

IV. LOOK BACK

i) In the process of solving the problem, you should have found two solutions. Are both solutions physically reasonable? Why or why not?

j) Compare and contrast the methods of physical experimentation and mathematics in solving projectile motion problems.

For Further Thought

In this Thought Project we confronted an equation that required us to use a technique called the quadratic equation. Before we leave this project, it is important to note that this is not the only mathematical technique that can be used to solve polynomial equations. Another powerful technique that can be employed to solve equations of this type is known as *factoring*.

Factoring

When we factor an expression, we break it down into a sequence of terms that are multiplied together. If we break down the expression correctly, we can regain our original expression by multiplying all of the terms in the sequence. For example, we can break down the number 6 into the product of the numbers 2 and 3:

$$6 = 2(3)$$

> 2 and 3 are called the *factors* of the number 6.

This procedure can be applied to expressions that contain variables as well as those with numbers. When we perform this technique, we say that we have *factored* the polynomial. However, when factoring polynomials, it is not always easy to determine what types of terms must be multiplied together. Let's take a few moments to learn the basics of factoring and to see how these techniques can be used to solve equations that might arise in problem solving situations.

Suppose that we have an equation such as:

$$x^2 + 8x + 12 = 0$$

We know that we can solve it using the quadratic formula. Using that formula, we find that the solutions to the equation are x = –2 and x = –6. It is possible, however, to use factoring to arrive at these same two solutions.

We can break the expression into two factors that, when multiplied together, will give us back $x^2 + 8x + 12$

$$(x+2)(x+6) = x^2 + 8x + 12$$

This means that if

$$x^2 + 8x + 12 = 0$$

then

$$(x+2)(x+6) = 0$$

If two terms are multiplied and yield an answer of zero at least one of the terms must be zero. In our example, we see that $x + 2 = 0$ or $x + 6 = 0$.

If we solve each of these two equations individually, we again produce the two solutions to this problem, x = –2 and x = –6.

Math Review

For a refresher on multiplying polynomials, reread Interlude III or consult your Tools book.

Read: Section 4.6

MathPro: 4.6A

Math Review

If you would like to learn more about factoring different types of polynomials and/or their applications to solving algebraic expressions consult your Tools book.

Read: Section 5.6

MathPro: 5.6A

> To summarize, when using factoring as an alternative method for solving quadratic equations, we factor the expression and then set each of the factors equal to zero. If we then solve these equations we will have the solutions to the original equation.

DRAWING SKILL OPPORTUNITY 8: DRAWING A PARABOLA

While this Thought Project focused on the motion of objects along the vertical axis, it is nearly impossible for an object in the real world to move purely along one axis. If we take into account the real world effects of wind, etc. the motion of projectiles is actually closer to the form of a parabola:

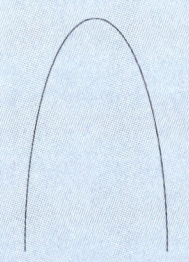

Figure 24.1 Symmetric parabola

The focus of Drawing Skill Opportunity 8 in Appendix A is to equip you with the requisite skills to draw this geometric figure. As you will see from both the commands given in the Drawing Skills section, and from your instructor, the height and width of the parabola are both easily controlled using the appropriate keyboard commands.

Thought Project 25
Factoring Puzzles

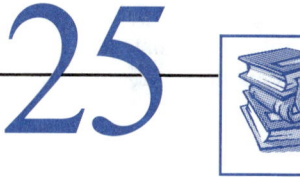

Skill Level I

In the "For Further Thought" section of Thought Project 24, we learned the mathematical skill of factoring. Factoring is a very useful problem solving tool because it allows us to make complex problems more approachable. Solving the factoring puzzles in this Thought Project provides an opportunity to practice this important problem solving skill.

Problem:

For each expression, factor each into two simpler expressions that can be multiplied together to generate the original expression.

1. $x^2 - 16$

2. $x^3 - 27$

3. $x^2 + 8x + 12$

4. $9v^2 - T^2$

I. UNDERSTAND THE PROBLEM

Do you understand all of the terms and the exact problem that you are being asked to solve?

Math Review

For a review and practice of factoring consult your Tools book.
Read: Sections 5.2 and 5.5
MathPro: 5.2A, 5.5C

Problem Solving Tips

Because you have been given the strategy "use factoring", you may proceed immediately to Carry Out the Plan.

II. CARRY OUT THE PLAN

a) Factor each expression and record your answers:

1.

2.

3.

4.

III. LOOK BACK

b) How can you check whether or not you have factored each expression correctly?

c) Identify some types of problem solving situations in which it might be advantageous to replace an expression with its factors.

Thought Project 26

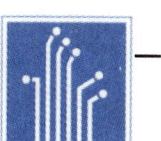

Working with Capacitors: Part A

All of the previous electronics Thought Projects in this text concerned only two components of a circuit—voltage sources and resistors. With this project we will encounter the *capacitor* which is another important element in a circuit.

A *capacitor* is an electronic device that stores potential energy in the circuit. It is usually made from two conducting surfaces that are placed close to one another. When the capacitor is wired with a voltage source, the flow of the current causes electrical charges to be stored on the plates of the capacitor. The result of the storage of charges is that an electric field is generated between the plates of the capacitor. And, more importantly for our purposes, a voltage difference appears across the plates of the capacitor.

Skill Level I

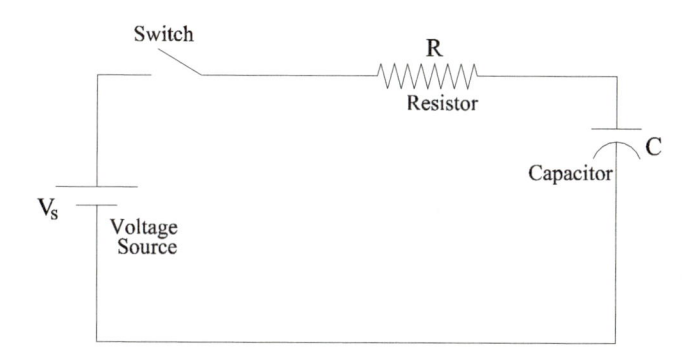

Figure 26.1 Charging capacitor

Unfortunately, the voltage that appears across the plates of the capacitor is opposite to the orientation (or *polarity*) of the source voltage. This opposite voltage caused by the charging capacitor fights the source voltage and causes the current flow to decrease. This means that the maximum current flow, I_{Max}, will occur when the switch in the circuit is first closed and the capacitor has not yet begun to charge. The current does not fall off in a linear fashion, but rather in an *exponential*

one. The current flow at any time t after the switch in the circuit is closed is given by the equation

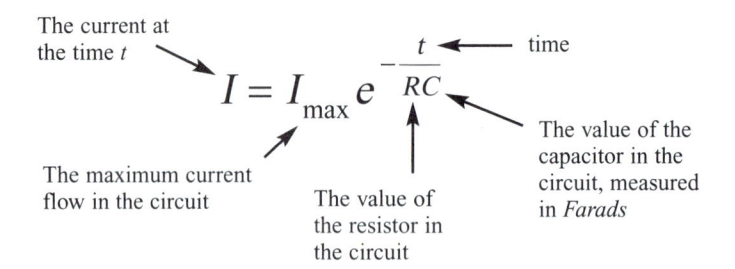

$$I = I_{max}\, e^{-\frac{t}{RC}}$$

- The current at the time t → I
- The maximum current flow in the circuit → I_{max}
- time → t
- The value of the resistor in the circuit → R
- The value of the capacitor in the circuit, measured in *Farads* → C

Problem:

If a circuit has a $3.9 \times 10^3\,\Omega$ resistor and a 5×10^{-6} Farad capacitor, find the current flow in the circuit at .005 seconds if the maximum current flow in the circuit is 1.5 Amps.

Use the problem solving skills you have learned to solve the problem.

Math Review

Read: Section 11.6 C, D
MathPro: 11.6 C, D

Skill Level II

Problem:

In this Thought Project, you are given the values of the resistor as well as the maximum current flow in the circuit. Construct a strategy that will predict the voltage source required to produce the maximum current given in the project.

a) Do the research necessary to determine whether or not this voltage is one that is normally available. If not, where might it be?

DRAWING SKILL OPPORTUNITY 9: DRAWING A SCHEMATIC SYMBOL

In this Thought Project, you were introduced to a new electronic device, the capacitor. Like its counterpart, the resistor, this device has a special symbol that represents it in a circuit schematic. Unfortunately the symbol for the capacitor cannot be drawn using simple straight lines like the resistor. Accordingly, in this Drawing Skill Opportunity you will be introduced to the appropriate commands to generate the schematic symbol for the capacitor.

Thought Project 27

Working with Capacitors: Part B

In Part A of *Working With Capacitors*, we investigated the current flow at a specific time. In this Thought Project, we will reverse the process and will learn how to find the specific time at which a given situation occurs.

Skill Level I

Problem:

If your circuit has a $3.9 \times 10^3 \Omega$ resistor and a 5×10^{-6} Farad capacitor, find the time at which the current flow in the circuit will be 1/2 of its maximum value.

I. UNDERSTAND THE PROBLEM

Make sure that you understand the terminology in the problem statement. If you do not, review the definitions, equation, and Math Review suggested in Thought Project 26.

II. DEVISE A PLAN

a) In this probelm, you are not given the value of the maximum current flow. Is there a way to eliminate it from the equation? Explain.

b) What is the exact form of the equation that needs to be solved?

Math Review

Read: Section 11.6
MathPro: 11.6 C, D

c) What mathematical techniques do you suggest for solving this type of equation?

III. CARRY OUT THE PLAN

d) Implement your mathematical strategy. At what time will the current flow be 1/2 of its maximum value?

IV. LOOK BACK

e) When executing your mathematical strategy, you probably calculated a logarithm that yielded a negative answer. In terms of the *physical* situation, why was this a necessity?

Skill Level II

Problem:

You have an RC-circuit with a direct current voltage source. If the resistor has a resistance of $6 \times 10^3 \Omega$, what value of capacitor would be required so that the current was at 1/4 of its maximum value in 0.00003 sec?

Skill Level III

In the language of electronics, the value of the resistor, R, multiplied by the value of the capacitor, C, is known as the *capacitive time constant*. This number, RC, is the amount of time we have to wait until the current has fallen to 37% of its maximum value.

> The **capacitance** of an object is defined as the ratio of the charge stored on the plates of the capacitor to the voltage across the plates. In equation form:
> $$C = \frac{q}{V}$$

Note that the units of capacitance can also be expressed as Coulombs/Volts.

Problem 1:

Demonstrate that the units of resistance (measured in Ohms) multiplied by the units of capacitance (measured in Farads) yield the units of time (measured in seconds.)

Problem 2:

Demonstrate why the capacitive time constant is the amount of time that is required for the current flow to reach 37% of its maximum value.

Thought Project 28
In Search of the Wooly Mammoth

In Thought Project 15, we were introduced to two topics from the field of genetics: the structure of a DNA molecule, and the concept of cloning. In this Thought Project, we will use these ideas as a springboard to a useful archaeological tool—radiocarbon dating.

In 1997, scientists discovered the frozen remains of a long extinct animal, the wooly mammoth. The body of the animal was so well-preserved by ice that scientists believe they will be able to extract a sample of DNA from it and clone a replica. If they are successful, a long extinct animal will once again appear.

While the actual topics of genetics and cloning were the focus of Thought Project 15, our focus here is on the technique that the archaeologists used to date the animal—radiocarbon dating.

Our study of this procedure places us in an interesting position. Up to this point in our problem solving studies, we have only dealt with atoms and the electrons that orbit in the outer regions of the atom. For us to understand radiocarbon dating, we must dig deeper into the atom and look at its center. This central portion of the atom is called the *nucleus*.

The nucleus of an atom contains two types of particles—protons and neutrons. The number of each of these particles conveys the information that we need to understand this archeological dating technique.

The number of *protons* inside the nucleus determines the *element*. For example, all atoms that have a total of eight protons inside their nucleus are called oxygen, all atoms that have a total of six protons are called carbon.

Where the number of protons determines the element, the number of *neutrons* determines the version (or *isotope*) of the element. An example of this isotope concept is the element carbon. The atom that has six protons and eight neutrons is called carbon–14, while the atom that has six protons and six neutrons is called carbon–12. The number that is attached to the carbon comes from adding the number of protons and the number of neutrons together. Since they both have a total of six protons, each is carbon. The differing number of neutrons classifies them as different isotopes of the element carbon.

In addition to having different numbers of neutrons, the two carbon isotopes behave very differently. The nucleus of a carbon–12 atom is very stable while the nucleus of a carbon–14 atom is not. This instabil-

A rendering of the now-extinct wooly mammoth.

Courtesy of J. Blair

ity causes the nucleus of carbon–14 to change. Because the nucleus is radiating, it changes and no longer remains carbon–14. This changing carbon–14 is at the center of radiocarbon dating.

All living things, such as trees, people, and wooly mammoths, contain this radioactive isotope of carbon. By finding the amount of carbon–14 left in an archaeological discovery, scientists are able to backtrack and calculate when the animal, tree, etc., was alive.

The basic equation that the scientists use is

$$N = N_0 e^{-\lambda t}, \text{ where}$$

N is the amount of a material that is left after a certain amount of time, *t*.

N_0 is the initial amount of the material before it began to decay into other materials.

λ is the decay constant of the material. This is the amount of time required for the material to decay into other products.

t is the time at which you are looking at the sample.

Notice that the negative sign on the exponent has the mathematical meaning that we will have less and less of a radioactive sample as time goes along. This agrees with what we expect *physically* in this Thought Project.

Solve the following problems and show your work.

Math Review

Read: Section 11.6
MathPro: 11.6 CD

Problem 1:

If we have 5000g of a radioactive substance and it has a half-life such that we will have half of the original material left after 100 seconds, how much will we have left after 50 seconds?

Problem 2:

For the radioactive material in Problem 1, how long would we have to wait until 99% of the original material had decayed?

Problem 3:

Work with your partner to compose a list of important objects from the past. The criterion for an object making your list is that its date is of critical importance to our current understanding of the world. In other words, if we can attach a date to these objects, it will aid us in understanding our physical world. For each of the objects on your list, give a strategy for how you might attach a reliable date to it. Remember, an important object might be one year old, or 500 million years old!

I. UNDERSTAND THE PROBLEM

a) In your own words, write out what you interpret the problem statement to be asking. Compare your interpretation with that of others in your class.

b) In your interpretation, what are the key terms in the problem statement?

II. DEVISE A PLAN

c) Explain by what criteria you and your partner are judging the "importance" of an object.

d) For which historical objects would a determination of the radio-carbon dated age add significantly to our understanding of our world? Defend your choices.

III. CARRY OUT THE PLAN

e) For the objects that you listed in *d*, explain how you might attach a reliable date to each.

IV. LOOK BACK

f) For each of the methods that you listed in *e*, is there a way to quantify the amount of error associated with your dating technique? Explain.

Interlude IV

Unit Analysis

As we have found, technical problem solving is often a difficult process. The intuition and practical experience that is helpful in solving non-technical problems is often of no help in working technical ones. After acquiring experience in the field, technical intuition can be developed but it takes time and practice to become proficient. As beginning technical problem solvers, we need to acquire as many tools as possible to help us in this endeavor.

One such tool that can give guidance in solving technical problems is *unit analysis*. Analyzing the units in which quantities are expressed gives us access to a wealth of information about the setup and correct mathematical execution of the problem.

For example, in Thought Project 9 we worked with the equation $d = rt$. Because the distance is equal to the rate multiplied by the time, the *units* of distance must be the units of rate multiplied by the units of time. If we express the units of rate in meters per second, and the time in seconds, we can find the distance unit by multiplying the units together:

$$d = rt$$
$$[d] = \frac{meters}{sec} \cdot sec \quad \text{The seconds cancel each other leaving meters.}$$
$$[d] = meters$$

Another example draws on Thought Project 8 in which we learned the equation $Q = mL_f$. Although we were given the units for the latent heat of fusion in the project, we could have found the units on our own using unit analysis.

If we take the equation and isolate L_f we have

$$Q = mL_f$$
$$\frac{Q}{m} = L_f \quad \text{Multiply both sides by 1/m.}$$

This means that the unit of latent heat must be the units of heat (calories) divided by the units of mass (grams):

$$\frac{Q}{m} = L_f$$

$$\frac{cal}{g} = [L_f]$$

By using unit analysis, we reproduced the units of cal/g that were provided to us in the Thought Project.

Although the two previous examples were straightforward ones, they do not illustrate the full power of this tool. Its real advantage comes in more complex applications such as geometry and other more complicated equations. As an example, let's see how unit analysis can predict the dimensionality of a figure.

By analyzing the units on an expression, we can tell immediately whether the figure is one-, two-, or three-dimensional.

1) The *volume* of an object is the amount of three-dimensional space that an object occupies. Different geometric forms require different equations for finding their volume. Let's look at two different figures, calculate their volumes, and compare the results.

Example A–The volume of a cube

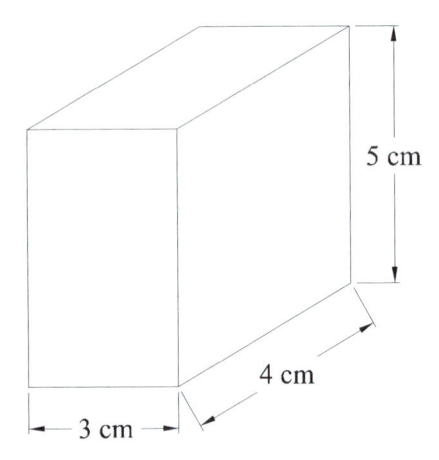

Figure IV.1

We can find the volume of a cubic figure by multiplying its length, height, and width together:

$$V = lhw$$

Placing all three variables, lhw, on the right side implies that they are to be multiplied.

Because we multiply, the units of volume must be the units of all three sides multiplied together. The key is that numbers stay with numbers and the units stay with the units:

Math Review

Read: Appendix A.5

$$V = (3\,cm)(4\,cm)(5\,cm)$$
$$V = (3)(4)(5)\,cm \cdot cm \cdot cm$$
$$V = 60\,cm^3$$

Notice that in the final answer, we have replaced cm•cm•cm with its simpler form of cm³.

Example B–The volume of a sphere

To find the volume of a sphere, we use the equation $V = \frac{4}{3}\pi r^3$, where r is the radius of the sphere. If we apply this equation to the sphere

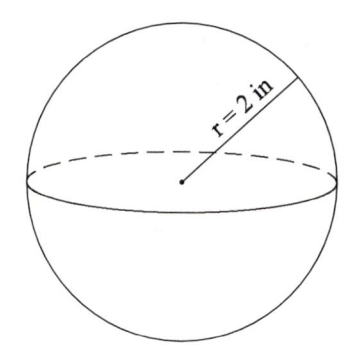

Figure IV.2 Sphere of radius 2 inches

we get

$$V = \frac{4}{3}\pi r^3$$
$$V = \frac{4}{3}\pi (2\,in)^3$$

Note that the exponent of 3 on the radius tells us that we are supposed to multiply 3 identical copies.

$$V = \frac{4}{3}\pi (2\,in)^3$$
$$V = \frac{4}{3}\pi (2\,in)(2\,in)(2\,in)$$

Once again, grouping numbers with numbers and units with units, we have:

$$V = \frac{4}{3}\pi (2\,in)(2\,in)(2\,in)$$
$$V = \frac{4}{3}\pi (2)(2)(2)\,in \cdot in \cdot in$$
$$V = \frac{32\pi}{3}\,in^3$$

If we compare Example A and Example B, we see that the units in both cases are a length unit raised to the third power. This is true of all three-dimensional figures. If the figure is three-dimensional, the units on its volume must be three length units multiplied together.

> **Math Review**
> Read: Appendix A.4

2) The *area* of a figure is the amount of two-dimensional space that an object occupies. Using a similar technique to that used with volumes, let's find the areas of two geometric figures and compare them.

Example C–The area of a rectangle

The area of a rectangle is found by multiplying its length by its width.

$$A = lw$$

If we use this equation to find the area of

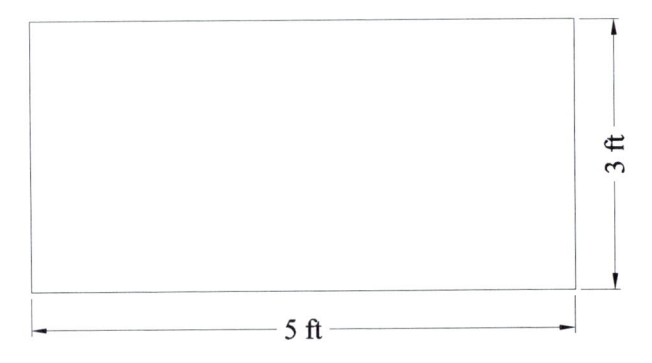

Figure IV.3

we have

$$A = lw$$
$$A = (5 \text{ ft})(3 \text{ ft})$$
$$A = (5)(3) \text{ ft} \cdot \text{ft}$$
$$A = 15 \text{ ft}^2$$

Notice that, once again, we have replaced the units of ft•ft with ft^2 using the rules of bases and exponents.

Example D–The area of a circle

We can find the area occupied by the circle

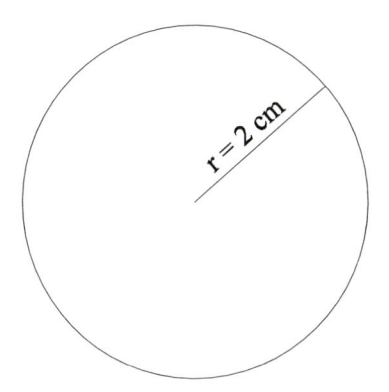

Figure IV.4

By using

$$A = \pi r^2$$

inserting the value of the radius and being careful to keep track of our units, we see that :

$$A = \pi r^2$$
$$A = \pi (2\,cm)^2$$
$$A = \pi (2\,cm)(2\,cm)$$
$$A = \pi (2)(2)\,cm \cdot cm$$
$$A = 4\pi\,cm^2$$

Notice that in both Examples C and D, the units on both areas are two length units multiplied together. To calculate the area for any two-dimensional object, we will always multiply two length units together.

Realizing that lengths are always measured in units such as inches, centimeters, miles, etc., we can now summarize our results.

- The volumes of three-dimensional figures are expressed as a length unit raised to the third power such as cm^3, in^3, ft^3, etc.
- The areas of two-dimensional figures are expressed as a length unit raised to the second power such as cm^2, in^2, ft^2, etc.
- One-dimensional figures are expressed as a length unit raised to the first power such as cm, in, ft, etc.

As a last note in this Interlude, remember that the technique of unit analysis will also let us move in the other direction. If we are given the dimensions of the area of a circle, for example, we can take a square root and find the units for the radius. Similarly, if we are given the units for the volume of the sphere, we can take a cube root and find the radius of the sphere.

Thought Project 29
Colors

Skill Level I

Do you have a favorite color? Are there colors that you find unattractive and would never consider wearing or using in your home? Do you ever think about the impact color has on your moods and impressions of things? Believe it or not, color plays such a significant role in our society that entire branches of scientific research are devoted to the study of color.

One of the interesting characteristics of color is that each color is produced by an electromagnetic wave of a different length.

For example, where the wave for one color may look like this,

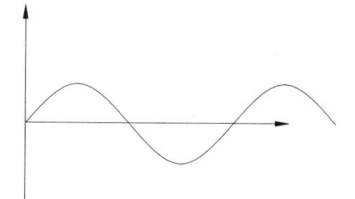

Figure 29.1

another takes the form of

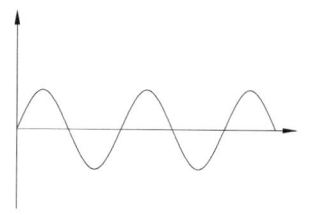

Figure 29.2

Because there are many different colors with varying wavelengths, we need to find a convenient method for summarizing this information. One method is to use a *graph*. In simple terms, a graph is a picture of quantitative information.

Let's graph the colors in the rainbow. The colors red, orange, yellow, green, blue, indigo, and violet represent the color spectrum. Look at the graph that lists the various colors of this spectrum according to their wavelengths:

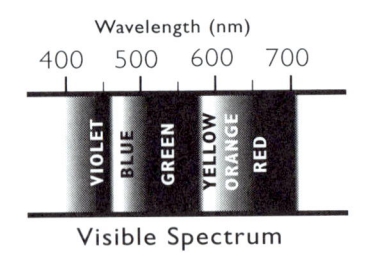

Figure 29.3 Visible spectrum

There are many different ways to graph data and interpret the data in the graph. The next graph is one that compares the wavelengths of various colors to the sensitivity of the human eye:

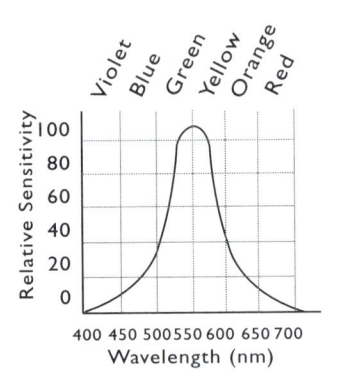

Figure 29.4

The human eye responds differently to various colors. For example, the peak of the graph corresponds to yellow-green. Our eyes are capable of discerning subtle differences in shades of green more easily than in those colors on the edges of the graph (red and blue). Studies have also shown that green is far less stressful on the human eye than are either red or blue.

Use the graphs to develop a strategy for solving the following problem.

Problem:

Design an experiment that uses color to modify human behavior.

I. UNDERSTAND THE PROBLEM

    a) Discuss how the graph of wavelengths vs. eye sensitivity relates to this problem.

    b) Write down a hypothesis for this problem.

II. DEVISE A PLAN

    c) Identify some possible strategies to test your hypothesis.

d) Are all the strategies that you listed in *c* equally viable? Do any of them appear to yield a solution to the problem more readily than others? If so, why?

e) In addition to the graphs given in this Thought Project, is there any additional data that would be useful or necessary to solve this problem and that you would need for your strategy?

f) If you answered yes to question *e*, what are some possible sources for this data?

g) To assist you in testing your hypothesis, do you feel that the data given in the graph could be illustrated differently? In other words, would a bar chart, pie chart, etc. be a better way to graph this data?

III. LOOK BACK

h) Discuss your opinion of graphing as a problem solving tool. When could it be used as an effective tool?

i) Discuss the outcome that you feel would result if your problem solving technique was applied to the problem in this Thought Project.

DRAWING SKILL OPPORTUNITY 10: SELECTING COLORS

Although the mathematical topic in this Thought Project involved reading graphs, the subject of the graphs themselves provide a perfect opportunity to learn another aspect of the software package.

In this skill opportunity, you will be shown how to change the colors of various layers of a technical drawing. Consult Appendix A for more information on this topic.

Thought Project
Semi-conductors

30

Skill Level

I

In several previous Thought Projects, we studied some of the quantities that affect the operation of an electronic circuit. In this Thought Project, we will look at a different aspect of electronics—namely the *conductivity* of the wire through which the current is flowing.

Simply, the conductivity of a material is a measurement of how easily the electric current is able to flow through the material. Some materials allow for a large current flow and others do not. By looking briefly at the atomic structure of wire, we can learn some of the reasons for the high or low conductivity of a material.

When the atoms in a material bond together to make solids, such as copper, silver, rubber, etc., all of the electrons in the atoms may or may not be necessary for the bonding process. The electrons that are necessary for the bonding process are tightly bound to the atoms and exist at lower energy levels than the electrons that are unnecessary. These low energy electrons are called *valence band* electrons. The term *band* arises from the fact that if we graph the energies of these electrons, they fall within a very narrow region on the graph.

In direct contrast, the electrons that are not necessary for the bonding process exist at higher energy levels than do the valence band electrons. These high energy electrons are free to move around in the solid if we close the switch in the circuit to provide a voltage. Because the number of these free electrons determines how well the material conducts electricity, they are referred to as *conduction band* electrons. Notice that the term "band" has again appeared. Like the valence band electrons, if we graph the energies of the conduction band electrons, they will fall into a narrow region on the graph.

We are now in a position to discuss whether a material is classified as an *insulator*, a *conductor*, or a *semi-conductor*.

1) *Insulators* have a large energy gap between the valence band and the conduction band. Consequently, a large amount of energy is needed to cause a valence band electron to move in a solid, thus adding to the material's conductivity.

2) In *conductors*, those electrons at the top of the valence band already have enough energy to move about in the solid if they are exposed to a voltage. A way to interpret this phenomenon visually is to think of it as having an overlap between the conduction band and the valence band on an energy graph of this material.

3) *Semi-conductors* are halfway between the two other types. There is still an energy gap between the valence band and the conduction band on an energy graph, but this gap is not nearly as large as it is in insulating materials. This means that through temperature increases caused by operation of the circuit, some valence band electrons can acquire the extra energy needed to jump up and become conduction band electrons.

Problem:

Construct an appropriate visual summary that compares and contrasts, in terms of the energies of the valence band and conduction band, whether a material is a conductor, an insulator, or a semi-conductor.

a) Is there a unique solution to this problem? Explain.

b) Are there visual constructions that would be more appropriate to solve this problem than others? What are some of these constructions?

c) Create your visual solution(s) to this problem in the space provided.

Thought Project 31

Who Is the Homerun King?

During the 1998 baseball season, the daily sports news was dominated by the home run race unfolding between Mark McGuire of the St. Louis Cardinals and Sammy Sosa of the Chicago Cubs. This homerun derby allows us to analyze a number of variables and to contrast the modern statistics with history. For example, how do we compare Mark McGuire, who now holds the record for the most homeruns in a season, with performances by Hank Aaron or Babe Ruth? Is it possible to compare the careers of these three athletes in an objective manner that yields useful information?

Mark McGuire, first baseman for the St. Louis Cardinals, broke the records for homeruns in a single season in 1998 with 70.

Copyright © AFP/CORBIS

Problem:

Acquire the necessary data, and compile it in an effective format to compare the batting careers of Babe Ruth, Hank Aaron, and Mark McGuire.

I. UNDERSTAND THE PROBLEM

a) In your opinion, what are the difficulties involved with making such a comparison?

b) What data do think you will need to compare the performances of these athletes in an objective manner?

Skill Level I

When there is a wealth of information, it is helpful to compile the data in a manner that summarizes the information and allows you to look for patterns in the data. These summaries frequently take the form of a *graph*.

> A *graph* is a table/picture that contains mathematical information.

II. DEVISE A PLAN

c) Identify some resources for acquiring the data that you need.

d) What type of graph do you think would be most effective for showing patterns in your data?

III. CARRY OUT THE PLAN

e) With the help of your instructor, construct a graph to summarize your data. If beneficial, construct more than one graph.

f) Now that you have graphed your data, do you think you need to do any additional research to make an objective comparison of Mark McGuire's, Hank Aaron's, and Babe Ruth's batting careers? If so, what is it?

g) Do your graphs show any patterns and/or trends? If so, discuss these patterns.

h) If you answered yes to *g*, what inferences can you draw based on the patterns you observed?

IV. LOOK BACK

i) What methods, if any, do you believe would be more effective than graphing for summarizing this type of data?

j) What types of problems might be most receptive to graphing as a problem solving technique?

Thought Project 32
HIV and the AIDS Virus

Skill Level I

Human Immune Deficiency Virus (HIV) and its full-blown counterpart, Acquired Immunity Deficiency Syndrome (AIDS), has reached the level of an epidemic. Recent data shows that approximately 95% of HIV-infected people live in the industrially developed world. Worldwide, an estimated 570,000 children (age 14 and younger) acquired the HIV virus in 1999. Further, experts estimate that by the end of the twentieth century, a total of 11.2 million children under the age of 15 were orphaned as a result of the AIDS virus.

Everyday we encounter media reports that update us on the progress of the fight against this epidemic. Although strides have been made, a cure still seems a long way away. What is it about this virus and disease that is so resistant to our problem solving techniques?

One of the answers to this question lies in the variable nature of the virus itself. Unlike polio and some of the other virus-borne diseases that challenged our forebearers, the HIV virus continues to change and show different forms and characteristics. Additional challenges involve the virus's crossing of age, gender, economic, and geographic boundaries and the many different ways in which the virus is transmitted.

It is this great variation that brings us to the subject of this Thought Project.

Problem:

1) Research information that you think would be necessary to address this epidemic.

2) With the assistance of your instructor, build several graphs to summarize the information that you have acquired.

I. UNDERSTAND THE PROBLEM

a) Write a detailed explanation outlining your interpretation of this problem.

II. DEVISE A PLAN

b) As you perceive the problem/epidemic, what types of statistics are necessary to help find a solution?

c) What sources will you consult to find these statistics?

III. CARRY OUT THE PLAN

d) Research the project and compile the necessary data. What do you think is the best method for summarizing the data you have acquired?

e) What types of graphs are most appropriate for the types of data that you have found?

f) With the assistance of your instructor, construct the appropriate graphs to summarize/compile your data.

Math Review
Read: Section 1.8
MathPro: 1.8 A, B

g) Do your graphs show any patterns or trends? If so, what are they?

h) After analyzing your data using graphical techniques, is there any additional research that you would conduct?

IV. LOOK BACK

i) In your opinion, is there a connection between different types of data and the graphical techniques used to summarize them?

j) Discuss graphing as a problem solving technique versus other techniques covered thus far.

Thought Project 33

How Warm Is It? Fahrenheit and Celsius

"It's 75° outside and a beautiful day." In the United States, we use the Fahrenheit scale to measure temperature. However, most of the world uses the Celsius scale. The Celsius scale is much easier to use because it is an evenly divided metric scale that establishes the freezing point of water at 0° and the boiling point at 100°. In contrast, the span of temperatures between the freezing and boiling point of water on the Fahrenheit scale is from 32° and 212°.

Skill Level I

Problem:

You are an American exchange student planning to study in Florence, Italy during the winter term. In preparation for your trip, you consult the Italian school's website to find out what the temperature is likely to be. However, the daily weather is given in the Celsius scale. Use the table to find a way to convert temperatures from the Celsius scale to Fahrenheit.

Water	Fahrenheit scale	Celsius scale
freezes	32°	0°
boils	212°	100°

I. UNDERSTAND THE PROBLEM

Read the problem carefully. It may be helpful to underline the key pieces of information that you need to solve the problem. Make sure you understand exactly what problem you are asked to solve.

172 Thought Project 33

> **Problem Solving Tips**
>
> Try graphing the data in the table with the temperature in degrees Fahrenheit, T_F, on the vertical axis and degrees Celsius, T_C, on the horizontal axis.

> **Math Review**
>
> Read: Sections 3.2, 3.3, 3.4
> MathPro: 3.3A, B 3.4 A, B

II. DEVISE A PLAN

a) What are some of the strategies you might use to find a solution to this problem?

b) Graph the information by drawing the coordinate axes with degrees Fahrenheit along the y-axis and degrees Celsius on the x-axis. Plot the information on freezing and boiling temperatures as points on the graph.

c) Devise a plan for how to use your graph to determine a relationship between T_F and T_C that can be used to convert Celsius measurements into Fahrenheit ones. Explain your strategy.

III. CARRY OUT THE PLAN

d) Execute your strategy and find a relationship between these two temperature scales.

e) Explain what the straight line on the graph tells us about the relationship between the two temperature scales.

f) In pure mathematics, when we draw a straight line through two points, we put an arrow on each end of the line to indicate that it continues infinitely in both directions. Would it be accurate to add arrowheads to the ends of the lines in our graph? Explain.

g) Is there a way to find the coordinates of the point on your graph that would be half way between the freezing point and the boiling point of water? If so, how?

IV. LOOK BACK

h) After having implemented your strategy, is there anything that you would do differently if you were confronted with the same problem? Explain.

Skill Level II

Problem:

Find a relationship that will allow you to go from a Fahrenheit measurement to a Celsius measurement in two ways:

1. By graphing the data in the chart given in Skill Level 1

2. By taking the relationship that you found in Skill Level 1 and algebraically manipulating it so that T_C is the dependent variable.

Discuss any advantages or disadvantages that you believe one strategy has over the other.

Another scale that is widely used by the scientific community is known as the Kelvin scale. This scale is based on absolute zero and thereafter is incremented in the same way as the Celsius scale. The temperature on the Kelvin scale can be found from the temperature in degrees Celsius by using

$$T_K = T_C + 273.15$$

Skill Level III

Problem:

If the temperature graph of a certain experiment formed a straight line when recorded on the Celsius scale, discuss what a graph of the same experiment on the Kelvin scale would look like.

Math Review
Read: Section 3.4
MathPro: 3.4D

Note
Unlike the other measurement scales, temperatures on the Kelvin scale are recorded using K not °K.

Thought Project 34

Global Warming and the Ozone

Skill Level I

As we enter a new millenium, the concerns about our environment and its care continue to grow. Because of political and lobbying efforts on the part of many environmental groups, great strides have been made in the United States and other parts of the world to combat this problem. Unfortunately, numerous industrialized countries have not made the necessary effort to protect our fragile environment. Too many nations continue to allow pollutants to be released into the world's atmosphere and water supplies at an alarming rate.

Two environmental issues that have received significant attention during the last 50 years are those of global warming and the hole in the ozone layer. As scientists investigate these two environmental phenomena, some effort has been made to show that these two effects are somehow related. What do you think? An investigation into possible relationships between these two environmental issues is the focus of this Thought Project.

Global Warming

The rate at which global warming is occurring is a controversial subject among scientists. Because scientists have only been studying the earth's weather patterns for the last century or two, it is difficult to make an accurate comparison of recent weather data to the overall weather patterns of a planet that has existed for millions of years. Consequently, it is hard to know whether rising temperatures are a cyclical phenomenon or a trend that could have devastating effects on our planet.

Very simply, global warming may be thought of as excess heat being trapped near the surface of the earth. Think about how hot a car becomes while parked in the sun on a summer day. The inside of the car is hotter than the surrounding air because the glass of the windshield allows the electromagnetic waves from the sun to pass into the car but does not allow the resultant heat back out. In a similar manner, the burning of fossil fuels (coal, oil, gasoline, etc.) on earth produces a layer of gases (commonly referred to as "greenhouse gases") that acts like the windshield of a car. This layer of gas allows the electromagnetic waves from the sun to pass through, but does not allow the heat from our planet back out into space. Many scientists argue that a prolonged build-up of heat could lead to the melting of the polar ice caps, raised oceanic levels, extensive flooding, and disastrous consequences to life on earth.

The Hole in the Ozone Layer

As we breathe, we take in a mixture of gases that includes life-sustaining oxygen. Actually, the oxygen that our body uses is formed of two oxygen atoms and is noted in chemical shorthand as O_2.

There is, however, another way for oxygen atoms to form into molecules. When three oxygen atoms bond together they form a molecule we call *ozone*—denoted as O_3. It is this type of molecule that makes up the ozone layer that surrounds the earth. This layer plays an important role in life on earth. Ozone provides a protective layer that shields the earth from the harmful, ultraviolet rays of the sun. Without this ozone shield, skin cancer levels would increase dramatically and the world's crop production would suffer devastating consequences.

In the last century, it was discovered that there were holes in the earth's vitally important ozone layer at both the north and south poles. Although the size of the holes changed during various times of the year, many scientists believed that these holes were being caused, at least partially, by fluorocarbons generated from spray cans and other man-made pollutants.

Problem:

To obtain funding for environmental research, you and a group of fellow scientists must develop a strategy for showing how a relationship may be demonstrated between the two atmospheric effects of global warming and holes in the ozone layer.

The following are possible relationships that might exist:

- Caused by the same thing
- One caused by the other
- Produce the same effect

I. UNDERSTAND THE PROBLEM

a) In your opinion, is there any sort of clarification that this problem requires in order to be solvable? Rewrite the problem, if desired.

II. DEVISE A PLAN

b) Discuss your initial problem solving strategy using your interpretation of the problem.

c) Do you think taking some actual physical measurements would yield helpful data? If so, what measurements are they?

d) How does your strategy compare to others in your class?

One way to obtain some useful data about how to relate these two effects is to examine where each exists in the atmosphere. Is the layer of gas that may be causing global warming close to the layer of ozone gas that protects us from the ultraviolet radiation? What does the word "close" mean in this situation? Also, how much total gas is in each layer? What is the total area that each layer occupies?

Problem Solving Tips
Draw a picture or diagram.

> **Math Review**
>
> To see a discussion of how to find the surface area of a sphere, or the area of other geometric figures, consult your Tools book.
>
> Read: Appendix A.5

e) Would such physical measurements benefit your proposed problem solving strategy? Why, or why not?

f) What are some sources for finding the data necessary to calculate the quantities that you think are beneficial to your problem solving strategy?

III. CARRY OUT THE PLAN

g) After you have done any necessary research, use the following chart to record your calculations and summarize your data.

	Distance from the surface of the earth	Distance from the center of the earth	Surface area of the sphere generated
Greenhouse gases			
Ozone layer			

IV. LOOK BACK

h) In the process of researching and making your calculations, did anything happen that you did not expect? If so, what?

i) What corrections to your initial problem solving strategy would you make if you were confronted with this problem again?

Skill Level II

Problem:

Find the names of the levels of our atmosphere, and their respective distances from the surface of the earth. Record your data in the following table. If the layer has a substantial thickness, record the distance range that corresponds to the layer:

Name of Layer	Distance

Thought Project 34

Hint

Consider whether or not the radius of the earth is important to this problem.

a) Calculate the surface area **and** the volume of the sphere that corresponds to the outermost edge of each layer of the atmosphere.

Name of Layer	Surface Area	Volume

Interlude V
Trigonometry

Throughout the book we have encountered a variety of geometrical topics. In some cases, we used geometry as the actual problem solving tool, and in others it allowed us to construct a diagram of the problem that confronted us.

In this Interlude, we will focus on a specific geometric form—a right triangle. As we will see in later Thought Projects, a thorough understanding of this simple geometric figure will provide us with a powerful tool.

Part I. The Pythagorean Theorem

Recall that a triangle is a closed figure that has three sides and three interior angles. Although we can have an infinite variety of interior angles and side lengths, in this Interlude we are interested only in those triangles that have a 90° angle as illustrated in Figure V.1.

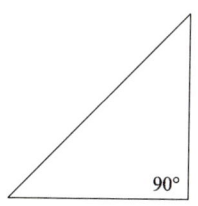

Figure V.1

By convention, we insert a small box in the corner to alert the reader that it is a 90° angle:

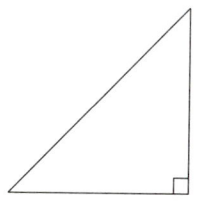

Figure V.2

Math Review
Read: Appendix A.6

Pythagoras (6th Century B.C.) Greek mathematician who studied the relationships between numbers and the sides of right triangles.

Courtesy of Pearson Education

Because leg *b* makes a right angle with leg *a*, this type of triangle is called a *right triangle*.

Our understanding of right triangles can be traced directly back to the work of a Greek mathematician named Pythagoras who showed that the lengths of the sides of any right triangle can be related to one another. He was able to show a mathematical relationship between the lengths of the sides *a* and *b* to the length of the longest side *c*:

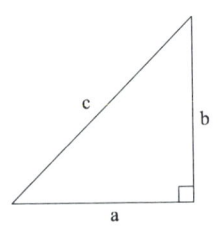

Figure V.3

The longest side, *c*, is always located directly across the triangle from the right angle and is called the *hypotenuse* of the triangle.

The mathematical relationship he demonstrated is referred to as the *Pythagorean Theorem*. It states that if we square the lengths of each of the legs, a^2 and b^2, and add them together, $a^2 + b^2$, we will always get the length of the hypotenuse squared. In equation form:

$$a^2 + b^2 = c^2$$

For example, if we have the following right triangle:

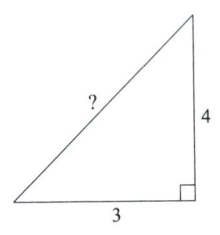

Figure V.4

we can find the length of the hypotenuse by employing the Pythagorean Theorem:

$$a^2 + b^2 = c^2$$
$$3^2 + 4^2 = c^2$$
$$9 + 16 = c^2$$
$$25 = c^2$$
$$\sqrt{25} = \sqrt{c^2}$$
$$5 = c$$

Note that we ignore the other answer to $\sqrt{25}$, namely −5, since a negative length would have no meaning here.

Problem:

Find the hypotenuse of the following right triangle:

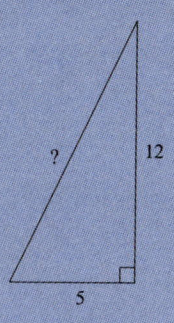

Part II. The Three Trigonometric Ratios

Future courses at ITT Technical Institute will make use of a set of remarkably powerful problem solving tools that can be found by relating the three sides of the right triangle to one another. This area of mathematics is known as *trigonometry*.

Let's look again at the right triangle shown in Figure V.4.

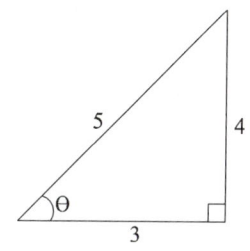

Figure V.6

Notice that this time we placed a symbol to represent the angle at the bottom corner of the triangle. This symbol is the Greek letter theta, θ, and is the variable that is most often used to represent an unknown angle.

Next we must assign names to the sides of the triangle. We already know the side of the triangle across from the right angle is called the hypotenuse. All that remains is to name the two legs of the right triangle.

The side of the triangle across from the angle of interest is called the *opposite side*. The remaining side of the triangle is called the *adjacent side* to our angle:

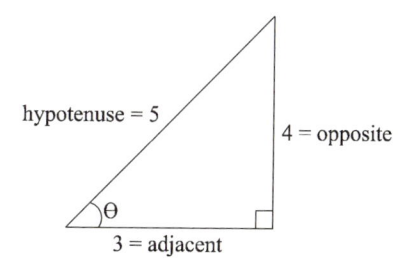

Figure V.7

Now that we have the names for the sides of the triangle, we can define ratios of one side to the other. We will assign a name to each of the ratios that we create.

1) The *sine* of the angle θ (written $\sin\theta$) is the ratio of the length of the opposite side to the length of the hypotenuse. In equation form:
$$\sin\theta = \frac{opp}{hyp}$$

2) The *cosine* of the angle θ (written $\cos\theta$) is the ratio of the length of the adjacent side to the length of the hypotenuse. In equation form:
$$\cos\theta = \frac{adj}{hyp}$$

3) The *tangent* of the angle θ (written $\tan\theta$) is the ratio of the length of the opposite side to the length of the adjacent side. In equation form:
$$\tan\theta = \frac{opp}{adj}$$

Using our previous right triangle, we see that our three trigonometric ratios become:
$$\sin\theta = \frac{4}{5}$$
$$\cos\theta = \frac{3}{5}$$
$$\tan\theta = \frac{4}{3}$$

Two more important points must be made about trigonometry:

1) Notice that if we had focused our attention on the top angle of our triangle:

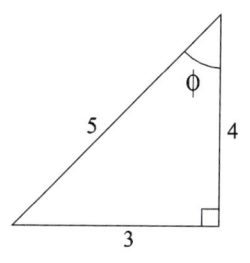

Figure V.8

the sides of the triangle that we identified as the opposite and the adjacent would become:

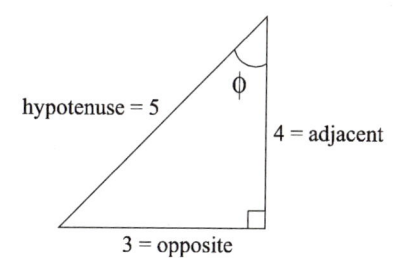

Figure V.9

for this angle,

$$\sin \phi = \frac{3}{5}$$

$$\cos \phi = \frac{4}{5}$$

$$\tan \phi = \frac{3}{4}$$

We used a different variable, the Greek letter phi (pronounced "fee"), ϕ, to represent the top angle. We need to use a separate variable since these two angles will almost always have different values.

2) Since the hypotenuse of the right triangle is always the longest side of the triangle, and is in the denominator of both the sine and cosine definitions,

$$\sin\theta = \frac{opp}{hyp}$$

$$\cos\theta = \frac{adj}{hyp}$$

the sine and cosine of any angle will always be less than or equal to one.

Thought Project 35
Billboard

A billboard painter has been assigned the task of changing the advertisement on a 20 foot billboard, the bottom of which is 15 feet off of the ground.

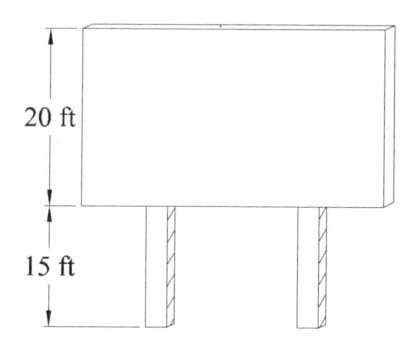

Figure 35.1 Billboard

After looking at the site, she sees that there are two areas on the ground that are sturdy enough to support the ladder. One area is 10 feet from the base of the billboard and the other is 15 feet from the base. To minimize the size of the ladder she must bring from her truck, she confronts the following problem.

Skill Level
I

Math Review
Read: Appendix A.6

Problem:

Which patch of ground will allow the painter to bring the shortest extension ladder and still have access to the bottom and top of the billboard?

I. UNDERSTAND THE PROBLEM

a) Draw a diagram of the problem.

II. DEVISE A PLAN

b) Discuss a strategy for solving this problem.

III. CARRY OUT THE PLAN

c) Execute your strategy and decide which patch of ground the billboard painter should choose.

d) By how much ladder length did the two patches of ground differ? Explain.

IV. LOOK BACK

e) In terms of the *physical* setup of the problem, is there anything that the painter should be aware of as she sets up her workspace? Explain.

Skill Level II

Problem:

Suppose that on the second day of the project, the painter is only able to bring a fixed-length ladder with her instead of an adjustable one. If she is only able to bring a 25 foot ladder on the second day, and places it on the patch of ground that is 10 feet away from the base of the sign, how far up from the bottom of the sign will she be able to place her ladder?

Thought Project 35

Skill Level III

One of the most widely used tools of astronomers is known as *parallax*. This tool is a method by which they are able to estimate the distances between stars, galaxies, etc. without having to leave the surface of the earth. This simple technique is based on the same principles reviewed in this Thought Project and taught in Interlude V on Trigonometry.

Problem:

Execute the necessary research and explain the principles behind, and uses of, the technique of parallax. Please be as detailed as possible in your discussion of both the theory and its uses.

DRAWING SKILL OPPORTUNITY 11: DRAWING A RIGHT TRIANGLE

In this Thought Project, we discussed how to find the lengths of the sides of a right triangle. This topic lends itself to another set of skills using the drawing software.

In this opportunity, you will again find the length of the hypotenuse of a right triangle. However the language you use will be very different. This skill is based upon using the software to find the distance between two points on your drawing.

Thought Project 36
Fiber Optics

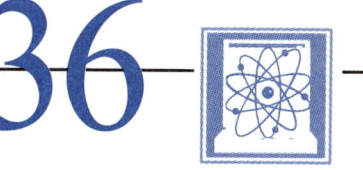

Have you noticed that a hand placed beneath the surface of the water in a swimming pool appears to bend at a bizarre angle at the wrist? This same optical illusion can also be seen if we insert a pencil halfway into a glass of water.

This optical effect is called *refraction* and is the basic principle behind fiber optics. Before studying fiber optics, we need to understand refraction and the equation that governs its behavior—Snell's Law.

Suppose that we aim a ray of light at the surface of a thick piece of glass. If we draw an imaginary dotted line perpendicular to the surface of the glass, we can measure the angle of the incoming light ray from this line:

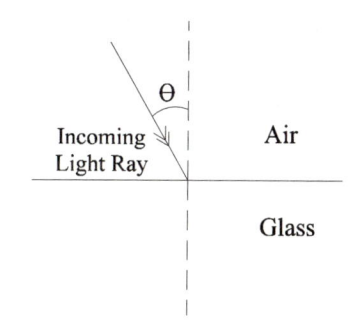

Figure 36.1

If we now follow the light ray into the glass, we see that it has bent closer toward the dotted line. The term we use for this bending property is *refraction* (Figure 36.2).

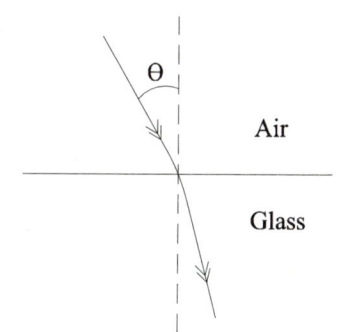

Figure 36.2

Skill Level

I

Because the material that the light entered in our example (the glass) was denser than the material where the light started (the air), the light was refracted toward the dotted line. This dotted line is usually referred to as a *normal line*. Because different materials have different densities, the angle that the refracted ray makes with the normal will depend on the material. The amount that the ray is refracted is controlled by a property of the material called the *index of refraction*.

The index of refraction of a material (normally given by the letter *n*) is the ratio of how fast light travels in a vacuum to how fast light travels in that material:

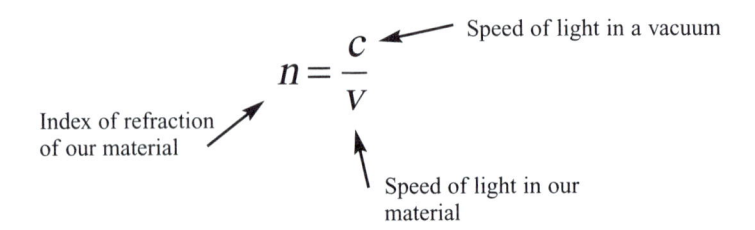

$$n = \frac{c}{v}$$

where *n* is the index of refraction of our material, *c* is the speed of light in a vacuum, and *v* is the speed of light in our material.

Notice that because both the numerator and the denominator of the right hand side are velocities, they have the same units. Because these units cancel one another, the index of refraction is a pure number with no units. A sample of the index of refraction for selected materials is as follows:

Table 36.1

Medium	Index	Medium	Index
Vacuum	Exactly 1	Typical crown glass	1.52
Air (STP)[h]	1.00029	Sodium chloride	1.54
Water (20°C)	1.33	Polystyrene	1.55
Acetone	1.36	Carbon disulfide	1.63
Ethyl alcohol	1.36	Heavy flint glass	1.65
Sugar solution (30%)	1.38	Sapphire	1.77
Fused quartz	1.46	Heaviest flint glass	1.89
Sugar solution (80%)	1.49	Diamond	2.42

Source: Halliday/Resnick/Walker, *Fundamentals of Physics* 5/e, John Wiley & Sons, 1997. Copyright © 1997 by John Wiley & Sons, Inc.

It is possible to relate the index of refraction of our two materials to the incoming angle and the angle of refraction. If we refer to the material in which the light ray started as #1 and the material that the light enters as #2:

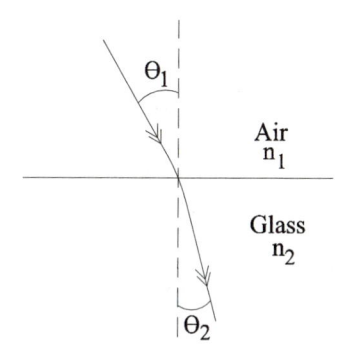

Figure 36.3

we can relate the two materials using *Snell's Law*:

$$n_1 \sin \Theta_1 = n_2 \sin \Theta_2$$

Example: A light ray in air (n = 1.00029) enters a piece of fused quartz (n = 1.46) at an angle of 30°. What angle will the light ray form with the normal line inside the fused quartz?

Solution:

To this point, we have examined situations in which a ray of light travels from a less dense material into a denser one. Another possibility is for a light ray to begin in a denser material and exit into a less dense material. What do you think happens to the angle of refraction in this case? In Figure 36.4 the light ray is bent farther away from the normal.

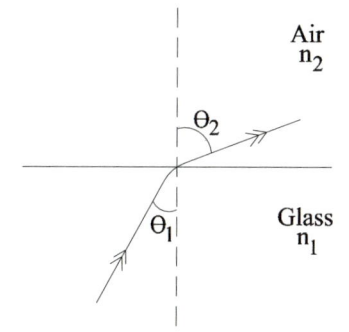

Figure 36.4

With this background on refraction, we are now ready to study fiber optics. Let's use Snell's Law to conduct a thought experiment. In our experiment the light ray begins to travel through a denser material #1 and then passes into a less dense material, #2. If we continue to increase the angle that the beginning ray makes with the normal, the refracted ray will move farther and farther away from the normal as in Figure 36.5.

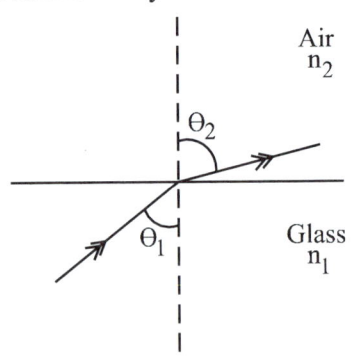

Figure 36.5

Let's continue to increase the initial angle until the refracted ray is bent so far away from the normal that it is actually along the interface between our two materials (Figure 36.5).

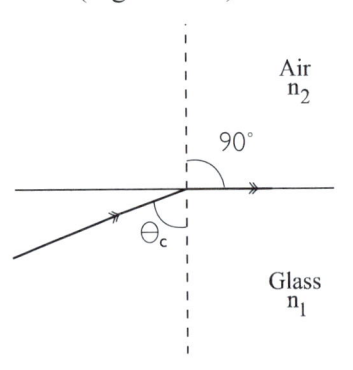

Figure 36.6

The initial angle that causes the refracted ray to move along the interface between our two materials is called the *critical angle*, Θ_C.

Any angle beyond this critical angle will now force the refracted ray to be reflected back into material #1. This effect is called *total internal reflection* and is the basis of fiber optics.

Let's use Snell's Law to describe the physical situation that we just described. If we begin with our initial equation:

$$n_1 \sin\Theta_1 = n_2 \sin\Theta_2$$

and insert the fact that we called Θ_C the angle required to cause total internal reflection and that Θ_2 must be 90° (because the refracted ray is measured from the normal), we get

$$n_1 \sin\Theta_C = n_2 \sin 90°$$

Because sin 90° = 1 (verify on your calculator):

$$\Rightarrow n_1 \sin\Theta_C = n_2$$

Dividing both sides by n_1:

$$\sin\Theta_C = \frac{n_2}{n_1}$$

This equation is an example of how mathematics can give us profound physical information. Because the sine function can never be greater than one, this forces

$$\frac{n_2}{n_1} \leq 1$$

This means n_1 must be greater than or equal to n_2. In other words, we can only achieve total internal reflection if the material in which the light ray starts has a greater density than the material that the light ray is entering.

Problem:

Using the information given in this Thought Project, do the necessary research and give a detailed explanation of how fiber optic cables are able to carry light waves and information.

Thought Project 36

I. UNDERSTAND THE PROBLEM

a) Is there a way to break this problem down into smaller pieces? Explain.

Math Review

If you need a refresher on inequalities and trigonometric concepts, consult your Tools for Problem Solving Text:

Read: Section 1.1

MathPro: 1.1A

II. DEVISE A PLAN

b) How might you approach the research necessary to solve this problem?

c) What are some of the key pieces of information that are required in order for you to give a detailed explanation of fiber optic cables?

d) Are there diagrams that you can construct that will help in your explanation? If so, what are they?

III. CARRY OUT THE PLAN

e) Record your explanation below. Attach additional sheets if necessary.

Thought Project 37
Lightning and Thunder

It is not uncommon to see something happen and then hear the sound from the event later. A familiar example is that of seeing lightning strike but not hearing the thunder for an appreciable amount of time later. Why is it that the action is not "in sync" with the sound?

We can explain this strange phenomenon with the science of waves. Whether it is a wave in the ocean, a wave on a rope, or an electromagnetic wave (such as the light from our sun), all waves take a certain time period to move from point A to point B.

An example of a normal lightning strike. Although it appears that the lightning originates from a cloud formation, the beginning of the weather phenomenon known as lightning actually starts on the ground.

Courtesy of Jeffrey M. Hamilton/Liason Agency, Inc.

Skill Level I

Problem:

Part 1: Construct a physical explanation for why the sound of thunder from a lighting strike appears after the actual bolt of lighting is observed.

Part 2: Devise and execute a strategy that would allow you to determine how far away from you the lightning struck, given that there was a five second time difference between when you saw the lightning and when you heard the thunder.

I. UNDERSTAND THE PROBLEM

a) What are the key pieces of information in these two problem statements? If desired, rewrite them in your own words.

b) In your opinion, would it be better to approach these two problems separately, or as one large problem? Explain your reasoning.

c) Do you have all of the information you need to solve the two parts of the problem? If not, what additional information or clarification do you need? Research any missing information and then proceed.

II. DEVISE A PLAN

d) For Part 1, state your explanation for the difference in time between when lightning is observed and the thunder is heard. How does it compare to that of others near you in class?

e) For Part 2, describe your problem solving strategy for finding the distance between you and the lightning strike.

f) Do the facts in the Hint about the speed of light and the formula for calculating the speed of sound suggest that you should modify your initial problem solving strategy? If so, how?

> **Hint**
>
> The following facts may be helpful in solving Part 2 of the Problem:
> - The velocity of light is approximately 3.0×10^8 meters per second.
> - The velocity of sound depends upon the temperature of the air through which the sound wave moves. With the temperature expressed in Celsius, the velocity of sound (in meters per second) can be found using the formula
> $v = 331 + .6T_C$.

> **Math Review**
>
> To help you quantify the difference in the time interval for this problem, you may want to consult the following sections in your Tools for Problem Solving Text.
>
> Read: Section 8.2,
> MathPro: Section 8.2A

III. CARRY OUT THE PLAN

g) Implement your strategy and find the distance between you and the lightning strike.

IV. LOOK BACK

h) How effective was your method? Do you believe your approach is the best strategy to solve the problem?

Thought Project 38

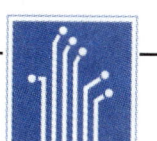

Alternating Current

In the last three Thought Projects, we will turn our attention to another important area of electronics–alternating current. The previous electronics Thought Projects dealt with circuits in which the current was only flowing in one direction. In circuits that have an alternating current (such as those in the home) the current switches direction back and forth with a set frequency. Our purpose here is to provide a brief introduction to this type of circuit in a problem solving context.

Let's begin our study of alternating current by looking at the power generated by the electric companies. Even though we are now concerned with alternating current, we can still express the power generated by the power plant as $P = IV$. However, in this situation we must be careful to use average quantities.

In Thought Project 18, we learned that the power dissipated by a resistor is given by $P = I^2R$. This equation continues to hold even though we are now using an alternating current. Because the transmission lines that carry the power sent by the electric company have resistance, power will be lost during the transmission process. These losses, which are dependent on the amount of current flow and the resistance of the transmission line, are called *Ohmic losses*.

Although some power loss is inevitable, the power equation, $P = IV$, provides a way to minimize these losses. Because the power generated by the plant is equal to the current flow caused, multiplied by the voltage caused, we can make the current flow very small by making the voltage very large. Having a small current will result in small Ohmic losses. A device that takes an existing voltage and either increases it or decreases it is called a *transformer*.

Skill Level

I

Note

You will learn about what it means to find the average value versus the root mean square (or **rms**) value of quantities in later coursework.

To create a transformer, we take two sets of wire and wind them around an iron core, as illustrated in Figure 38.1:

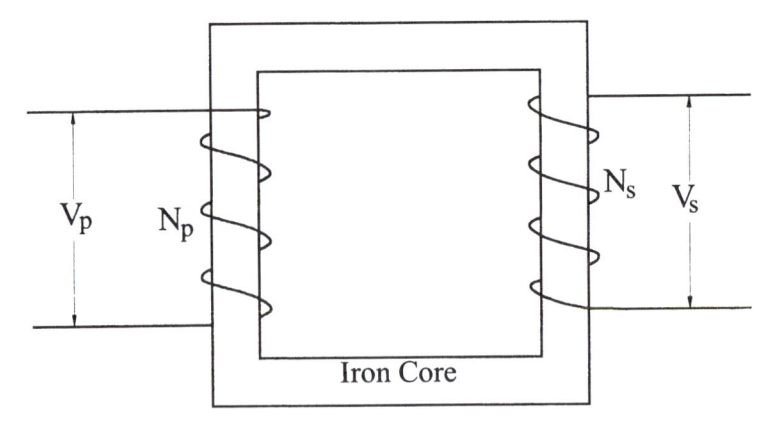

Figure 38.1

The left-hand side, called the *primary*, is the original voltage. The *secondary* is the new voltage that is created after being modified by the transformer. This secondary voltage is induced because of the alternating current in the primary. The alternating current in the primary causes an ever-changing magnetic field to appear inside the primary windings. This changing magnetic field is felt all through the iron core. Specifically, the changing magnetic field inside the secondary windings induces an alternating current in the secondary, as well as a secondary voltage.

The primary voltage, the number of turns in the primary, the secondary voltage, and the number of turns in the secondary can all be related by

$$\frac{V_P}{V_S} = \frac{N_P}{N_S}$$

Notice from our equation that if $N_S > N_P$, the new, secondary voltage will be larger than the original, primary voltage. Because the voltage has been increased, this is called a *step-up transformer*.

Conversely, if $N_S < N_P$, the secondary voltage is forced to be less than the primary voltage. This is known as a *step-down transformer*.

Problem:

Develop a strategy by which a power plant can produce a moderate and affordable power, transmit it as effectively as possible, and have it still be usable by a standard household on the receiving end.

a) Are there different stages to this problem? If so, discuss them.

b) Are there key pieces of information that you feel are necessary to solve this problem effectively? Explain.

c) Where might you be able to find these pieces of data?

d) Execute the necessary research, and write out a detailed solution to the problem. Use real world numbers that apply to your local school and home.

Thought Project 39
Independent Electronics Research

One of the determining factors as to whether a technician is successful or not in today's technological workplace is his/her ability and willingness to learn new concepts without the aid of an instructor or trainer. In an educational setting, it would be impossible to acquaint a student with every possible circuit configuration and electronics application. Because the technology field changes so rapidly, today's technician must be willing to read journals, textbooks, etc. to stay abreast of changing terminology, new technology, and myriad other pieces of information. In the workforce, one cannot rely on peers to teach the new developments in your field, self-reliance is required.

In this project, you are challenged to do the independent research necessary to acquaint yourself with a variety of electronics terms and devices without the aid of an instructor's lecture. In addition to illustrating the necessity of such independent research, this project provides a setting in which you acquire an introduction to several of the electronic devices that you will be studying at ITT Technical Institute.

The skill levels for this problem are determined by the number of terms correctly defined.

    Skill Level   I   1–15 terms

    Skill Level   II   2–20 terms

    Skill Level   III   3–25 terms

Thought Project 39

Problem:

For each of the following electronic terms and devices, find and write out an explanation of it *in your own words*. If it is an electronic device, include the standard way(s) of drawing the circuit element in a schematic. Include the units on the term and the variable that is used to represent it whenever appropriate.

1) resistor
2) current
3) voltage
4) electric charge
5) capacitor
6) switch
7) inductor
8) transformer
9) direct current
10) alternating current
11) inductive reactance
12) capacitive reactance
13) impedance
14) conductor
15) insulator
16) semi-conductor
17) power
18) pn-junction
19) depletion layer
20) transistor
21) operational amplifier
22) differential amplifier
23) Thevenin's Theorem
24) Kirchoff's Voltage law
25) Kirchoff's Current law

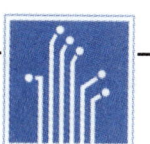

Thought Project 40
Impedance and Trigonometry

Skill Level I

The goal of this last Thought Project is to integrate many of the mathematical and electronic problem solving tools that we learned in the course. Along the way, we will draw upon a variety of previous mathematical tools, as well as previously discussed electronics topics. Because the focus of this course is to acquire new problem solving skills and refine those already acquired, this final project offers little guidance in solving the given problems. Although the problems are organized in a logical and necessary order, no other problem solving hints are given. The setting for this course wrap-up is the RLC circuit.

The RLC circuit

An RLC circuit contains a resistor, a capacitor, an inductor, and an alternating current voltage source (V_{AC}) all wired in series. This circuit provides a setting to analyze many interesting concepts in circuit analysis and to gain a deeper understanding of electronic effects that arise because the current is changing directions.

Problem 1:
Draw the appropriate schematic for an RLC circuit.

Electric current provides the means by which capacitors charge, thus causing an electric field to appear between its conducting plates. Also, electric current through an inductor causes the magnetic field in its center that enables the inductor to store potential energy. In this circuit we are dealing with an *alternating* current in which the directions of the fields inside both the capacitor and the inductor are constantly changing. The rate at which these fields change their *polarity*, depends upon the frequency at which the circuit is being driven with the alternating source. Unfortunately, nature opposes such changes. Accordingly, there is an opposition that appears in both the capacitor and the inductor. This opposition is analogous to the resistance in a resistor, and is known as *reactance*. Because we have opposition in the capacitor, we have a *capacitive reactance*, and because we have opposition in the inductor, we have an *inductive reactance*. Capacitive reactance and inductive reactance are usually expressed as X_C and X_L, respectively.

We can find the total amount of opposition that the circuit is providing to the alternating current by taking into account the resistance in the resistor, the capacitive reactance in the capacitor, and the inductive reactance in the inductor. This total amount of opposition is known as the *impedance* in the circuit. Impedance is expressed using the variable Z.

Because of their different construction, and the physical reasons why each provides a different portion of the impedance, the voltages across the three circuit elements are not in phase with one another. As the voltage source changes back and forth from negative to positive, the voltage across the inductor reaches its maximum value 90° ahead of when the maximum value of the voltage is achieved across the resistor. Likewise, the maximum voltage across the resistor is achieved 90° ahead of when the voltage across the capacitor is reached.

Problem 2:

Explain the phase relationship between when the maximum voltage across the inductor is achieved versus when the maximum voltage across the capacitor is achieved.

Problem 3:

Using arrows to represent the voltages across the three circuit elements, draw a graph that gives an accurate visual representation of the relative phases between the voltages across the three circuit elements. Assume that $V_L > V_R > V_C$ and make your graph to scale.

Problem 4:

Using Kirchoff's Voltage law, explain the relationship between the voltages that you inserted into your graph and the source voltage. Devise a way to insert the alternating voltage source, V_{AC}, into your graph.

Problem 5:

Because both V_L and V_C have the same units, is there a way to combine them in your graph? Explain. Redraw your graph if you were able to combine these two terms.

Problem 6:

Devise a way to construct a right triangle from the variables on your graph. Redraw your graph with this triangle included.

Problem 7:

Using the graph and its newly formed right triangle, devise a method by which the source voltage, the voltage across the resistor, the voltage across the inductor, and the voltage across the capacitor, can all be related to one another using an equation.

Problem 8:

Using Ohm's Law, we can write the voltages across each of the circuit elements as:

$$V_R = IR$$
$$V_L = IX_L$$
$$V_C = IX_C$$

Note that in the last two equations the reactances are playing a role analogous to our resistance.

Use these three equations coupled with the alternating current version of Ohm's Law: $V_{AC} = IZ$, to find an equation for the total impedance in the RLC circuit.

Skill Level II

Problem:

For simplicity we assumed that $V_L > V_C$ when we first introduced the problem. In this skill level, reverse this assumption and start with an RLC circuit such that $V_C > V_L$. Make the necessary diagrams, use the appropriate mathematical tools, and give a full explanation as to how this new assumption would affect the results that were found in Skill level 1.

As you will learn in later coursework at ITT Technical Institute, both X_C and X_L are dependent upon the frequency of an alternating source voltage. Accordingly, it is possible to find a frequency such that $X_C = X_L$. The frequency that will allow our two reactances to be equal is called the *resonant frequency* for the circuit.

Skill Level III

Problem:

Discuss how the amount of electric current in the RLC circuit would be affected by adjusting the input frequency so that it was the resonant frequency.

Appendix A

Drawing Skill Opportunities

Drawing Skill 1: Drawing Circles in a Rectangle
Drawing Skill 2: Drawing a Simple Circuit
Drawing Skill 3: Drawing Triangles
Drawing Skill 4: Drawing Pipes
Drawing Skill 5: Drawing a Parallel Circuit
Drawing Skill 6: Using the Explode Command
Drawing Skill 7: Drawing a Circle Inside a Circle
Drawing Skill 8: Drawing a Parabola
Drawing Skill 9: Drawing a Schematic Symbol
Drawing Skill 10: Selecting Colors
Drawing Skill 11: Drawing a Right Triangle

Drawing Skill 1: Drawing Circles in a Rectangle

This Drawing Skill Opportunity provides step-by-step instructions for creating a drawing of a circle placed inside of a rectangle.

Drawing a rectangle:

1. Select the Basic Drawing Template on the General Tab of the New Drawing Dialog box.
2. With your left mouse button, click on the Rectangle shape.
3. Holding the button down, drag the rectangle into the drawing editor
4. To resize the rectangle, click on it with the left mouse button, select one of the corners and stretch to the desired size.
5. At this stage, you will have created a complete rectangle on the draw screen.

Inserting a circle into the rectangle:

1. Using the mouse, single click on the circle, and holding down on the left mouse button, drag the circle into the drawing of the rectangle.
2. At this point, you should have a rectangle on your screen with a circle inside of it.

If you recall, the problem that confronted us in the Introduction to Problem Solving concerned the number of circles that could be placed inside of a certain rectangle. Using the drawing software, it is possible to get an approximation to this answer. We can now move the circle that we just created and begin inserting others.

Moving the circle:

1. To move the circle, click on it with the left mouse button, hold the button down, and move the circle to the new location.

Drawing Skill 2: Drawing a Simple Circuit

In this Drawing Skill Opportunity, we will learn how to draw the simple circuit that was the focus of Thought Project 1. We will begin with the battery and move clockwise around the circuit.

Drawing a battery:

1. From the new drawing dialog box, Click on the Electrical tab and choose the Electronics template. See Figure 1.

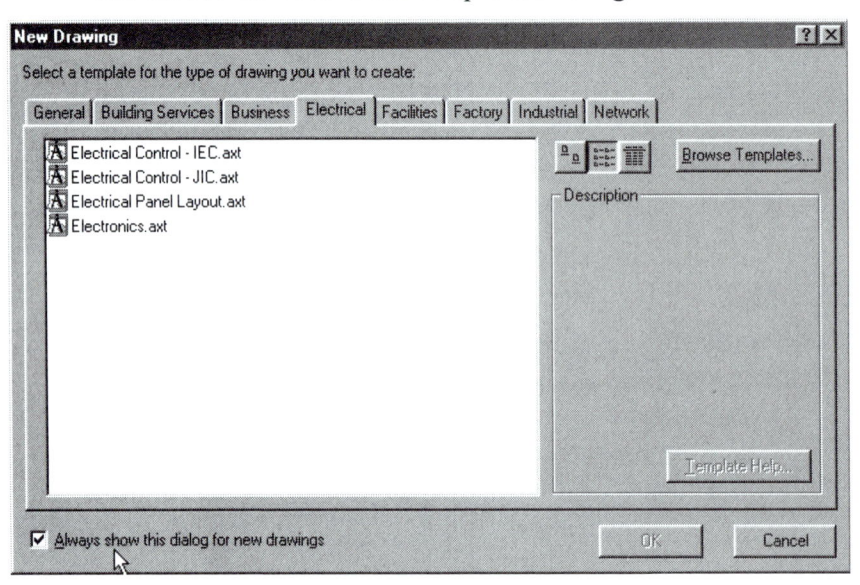

Figure 1

2. From the Content Explorer, Click on the menu pull down button and select Misc components as shown in Figure 2.
3. Select the multi-cell batteries symbol, and drag it to your drawing.

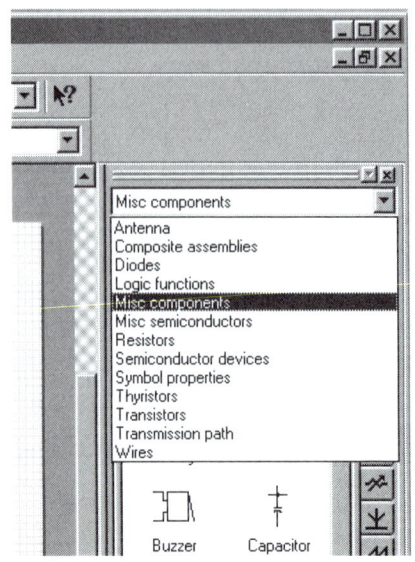

Figure 2

Adding the resistor:

1. From the Content Explorer, Click on the menu pull down button and select Resistors. See Figure 3.
2. Select the Series Resistor and drag it to your drawing. Next the Resistor will need to be rotated, select the resistor and right click to bring up the properties dialog box. Select rotate on this menu. See Figure 4. Rotate the resistor to the vertical position shown in Figure 5.
3. To draw the connection lines use the Connector Tool located on the main menu.

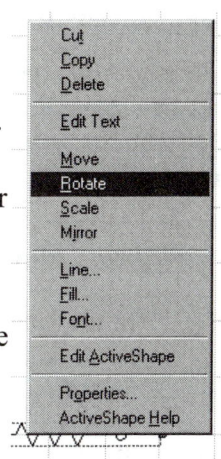

Figure 3

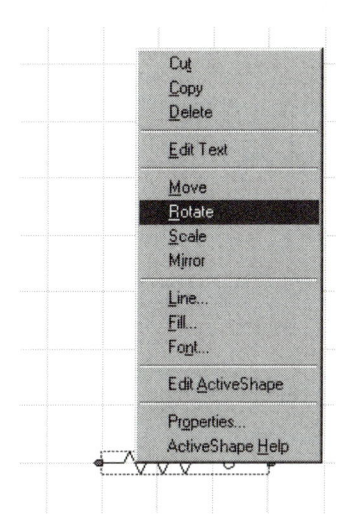

Figure 4

Select the Connection Tool, select the end of the resistor, and then select the end of the battery. A line will be formed between each of the components. Use the same procedure to complete the schematic drawing shown in Figure 5.

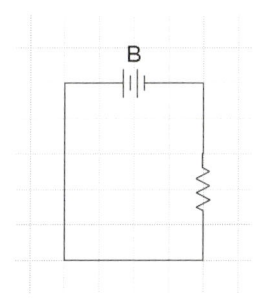

Figure 5

Drawing Skill 3: Drawing Triangles

Although there are many different angles from which to view the exterior of a pyramid, we will examine the front face in this Drawing Skill Opportunity. Although it may appear complex, drawing this view of a pyramid is nothing more than an exercise in drawing triangles.

Drawing an equilateral triangle:

1. In the New Drawing Dialog box, Select the General Tab and the Basic Drawing Template.
2. Select the Triangle from the Content Explorer and drop into the drawing.
3. To change the size, select the triangle, select the green corner and stretch to the new size.

Drawing Skill 4: Drawing Pipes

There are many methods for drawing pipes of varying widths, lengths, etc. The following sequence of commands is one of a number of sequences that will generate pipe drawings.

Drawing a pipe:

1. Select the Plumbing and Piping—Small Layout template from the Building Services Tab of the New Drawing Dialog.
2. Drag and Drop the Horizontal Pipe symbol into the drawing. Continue adding symbols to complete the drawing shown in Figure 1.

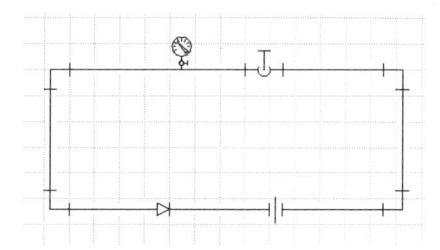

Figure 1

Drawing Skill 5: Drawing a Parallel Circuit

Our goal in this Drawing Skill Opportunity associated with Thought Project 14 is to use the drawing software to draw a circuit with three parallel resistors. This problem is an extension of the drawing we created in Drawing Skill Opportunity 2. This time, we will add two more resistors to our previous drawing. As a reminder, let's again look at the sequence of commands that we used to generate the battery drawing:

Drawing the battery:

1. From the new drawing dialog box, click on the Electrical tab and choose the Electronics template.
2. From the Content Explorer, click on the menu pull down button and select Misc components
3. Select the multi-cell batteries symbol, and drag it to your drawing and rotate it 90°.

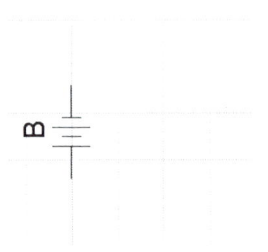

Adding the Resistor:

1. From the Content Explorer, click on the menu pull down button and select resistors.
2. Draw, drop, and rotate 3 resistors as shown below.

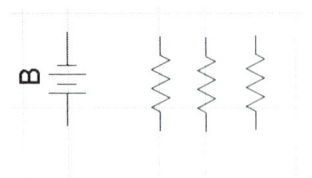

Drawing the wires that connect the battery and the resistors:

Select the Connection Tool, select the end of the resistor, and then select the end of the battery. A line will be formed between each of the components. Use the same procedure to complete the schematic drawing shown in below.

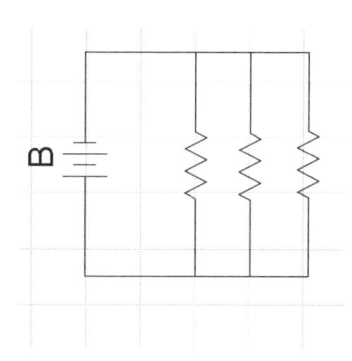

To add the connection points:

Use the circle icon to place a circle at each intersection and right click to bring up the menu. See Figure 1.

Select Fill and set fill color to black. See Figure 2.

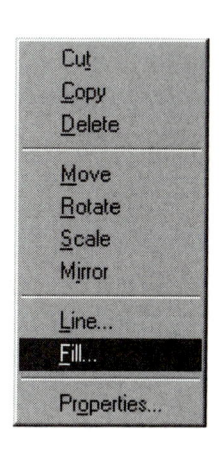

Figure 1

Figure 2

Your completed circuit should look like Figure 3.

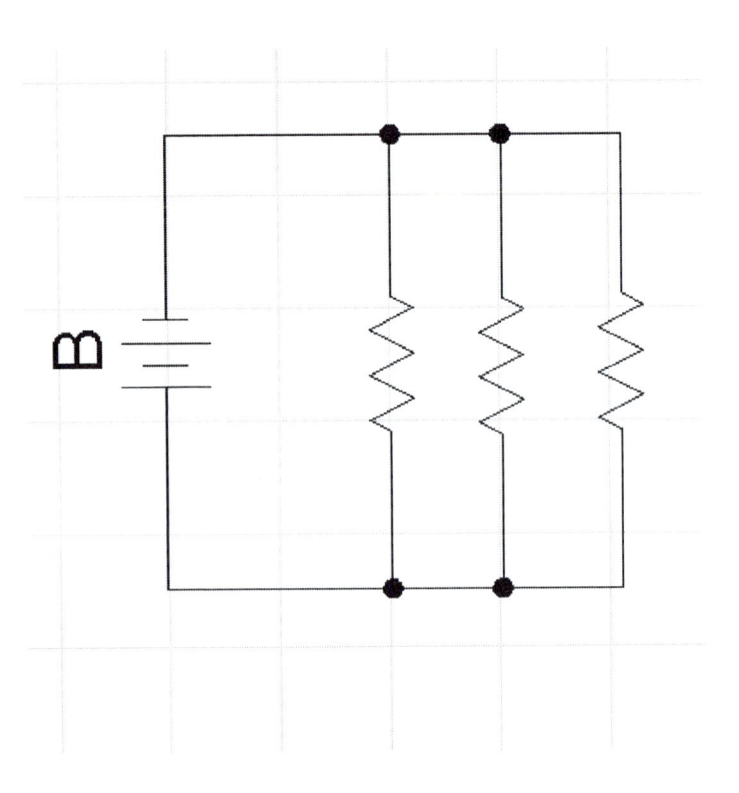

Figure 3

Drawing Skill 6: Using the Explode Command

Our goal in this Drawing Skill Opportunity is to acquire an introductory understanding of the Explode command. To understand the uses of this command, we must begin by opening our drawing from Drawing Skill 5.

Employing the Explode command:

1. Open the Parallel Circuit from Drawing Skill 5.
2. Click on the battery and select Modify and Explode from the pull down menu. See Figure 1.

By executing this command, you have now broken the battery into its different parts.

3. Select the "B" by the battery and press the delete key on the keyboard.

Your schematic should now look like Figure 2.

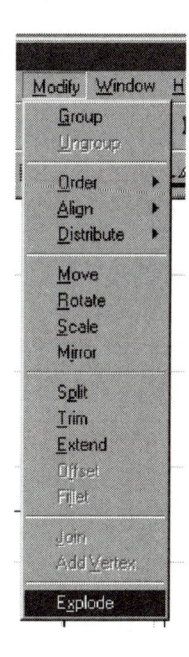

Figure 1

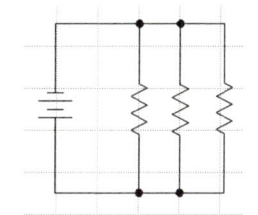

Figure 2

Drawing Skill 7: Drawing a Circle Inside a Circle

In this Drawing Skill Opportunity, we will use our drawing software to create a portion of the Power Wheel that was discussed in Thought Project 19. Recall that the Power Wheel contained both lettering and equations. Because this is intended to be only an introduction to the software package, we will not take on the more difficult tasks of inserting the equations or text that surrounds the outer portion of the wheel. These are advanced concepts that will be covered in later coursework at ITT Technical Institute. Instead, we will focus on inscribing circles.

We will accomplish this task thorough a three stage process. First, we will execute the commands necessary to generate the three circles. Second, we will insert the radial lines of the wheel. Lastly, we will insert the four letters P, I, V, and R into their respective locations.

Creating the three circles:

1. Select the Basic Drawing Template in the Create New Drawing dialog box.
2. Select the circle shape, drag it to you drawing and position it so that it is located approximately in the center of your screen.
3. Stretch the circle so that it has a radius of approximately 3/4 of an inch.
   We must now create the next largest circle. Our goal is to make this new circle have the same center as our first one.
4. Select the circle shape again and drag it to the center of the first circle. Notice that one circle "blocks out" the circle below it. Right click and set the fill for both circles to none.
5. Both circles should now appear on your screen.
6. Finally add the third circle.

Drawing the radial lines:

7. Draw a vertical and horizontal line trough the axis of the circle. See Figure 1.

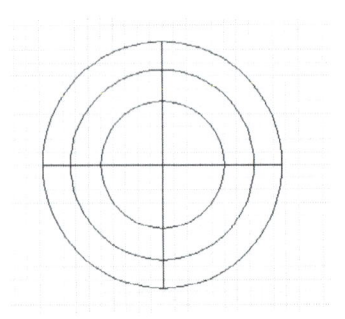

Figure 1

Inserting the letters P, I, V, and R:

8. Select the text and font size appropriate to your circle size and add the letters P, I, V, and R. Use the cursor to position your letters. See Figure 2.

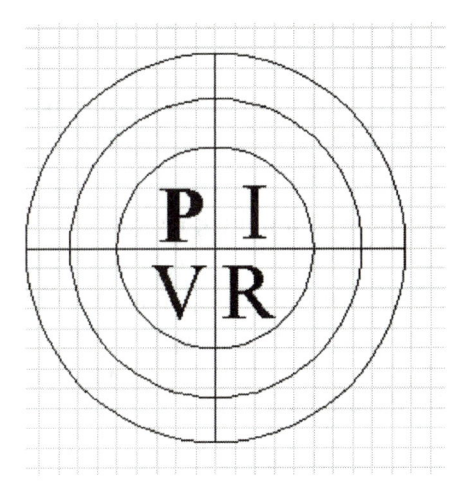

Figure 2

Drawing Skill 8: Drawing a Parabola

Now that we've completed Thought Project 23 and 24 on Projectile Motion, let's use the drawing software to draw the trajectory of one of our projectiles. Namely, let's learn how to draw a parabola. This exercise will use the Spline command.

Creating the parabola:

1. Select the Basic Drawing Template from the Create New Drawing dialog box.
2. Select the Spline Icon.
3. Begin by selecting grid points; try to make the curve as smooth as possible.
4. After the parabola is complete, convert it to an active shape by clicking on the Tools pull down menu and selecting Make ActiveShape. Select OK. You can now change the size and position of the parabola.

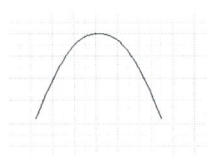

Drawing Skill 9: Drawing a Schematic Symbol

We have been adding resistors and batteries to our schematic, it is now time to look at a new component: the capacitor. If you return to Thought Project 26, you will see the symbol for a capacitor.

Adding the capacitor symbol:

1. Select the electronics template from the Create New Drawing dialog box.
2. From the Content Explorer, click on the menu pull down button and select Misc components.
3. Notice that we only have one capacitor, called *capacitor shunt*; this symbol will need some editing.
4. Drag the capacitor shunt into you drawing.
5. Right click on the symbol and select edit ActiveShape. Remove the "C" as well as the intersection and connection point.
6. Finally rotate the capacitor 90°. See Figure 1.

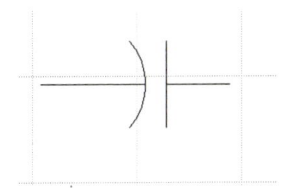

Figure 1

Drawing Skill 10: Selecting Colors

As with most software programs, colors can be easily added and changed in our drawings. In this Drawing Skill Opportunity, we will learn the commands that control the colors and thickness of objects in our drawings.

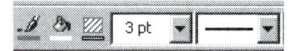

Figure 1

1. Figure 1 shows the toolbar items that control the color and thickness of objects in the Actrix software.

2. To draw a red line with a thickness of 3 pt, change the toolbar to the settings shown in Figure 1.

3. Draw several lines and circles of different colors and thickness as shown in Figure 2.

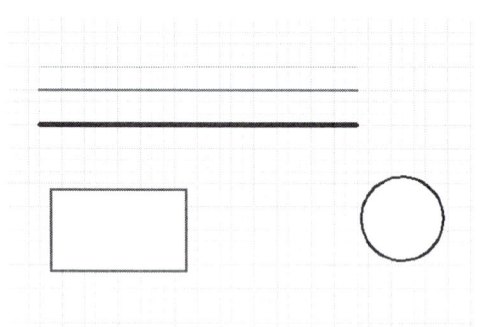

Figure 2

Additional opportunity:

If class time permits, return now to a Drawing Skill Opportunity of your choosing and rework it varying the colors of the shapes and lines that your drew.

Drawing Skill 11: Drawing a Right Triangle

The subject of Thought Project 35 provides a perfect setting to illustrate another useful property of the drawing software. In this Drawing Skill Opportunity, we will use the software to calculate the hypotenuse of a right triangle. By executing the appropriate commands, we may avoid the calculations associated with the Pythagorean Theorem.

This exercise has two components. First, we will draw the two legs of the right triangle. After they are created, we will find the length of the hypotenuse to complete the triangle.

Drawing the legs of the triangle:

1. Open the Basic Drawing Template from the Create New Drawing Dialog Box.

2. Select the Line icon from the toolbar.

3. Pick a point on the lower, left portion of the draw screen.

4. Count over 5 squares on the grid and select the point.

   (Side note: These steps may be somewhat familiar. If you recall from the Thought Projects on graphing, you always used a horizontal and a vertical axis. By selecting the point 5 units over and moving 0 units in the Y direction, you instructed the computer to make the line representing the bottom leg of the right triangle to achieve a length of 5 units out the *x*-axis, and 0 units up the *y*-axis.)

5. Now, to create the vertical leg of the triangle, again access the Line command.

6. Pick the point on the end of the horizontal line.

7. Count up 12 squares and pick the point.

At this point, you should have the two legs of your right triangle on the screen.

Creating the hypotenuse of the triangle:

8. Connect the end point of the vertical line to the end point of the horizontal line.

9. Count the number of squares that the angled line passes through. You should get 13. See Figure 1.

Let's now use the Pythagorean Theorem to verify that the software is correct:

$$a^2 + b^2 = c^2$$
$$5^2 + 12^2 = c^2$$
$$25 + 144 = c^2$$
$$169 = c^2$$
$$\sqrt{169} = c$$

It works!

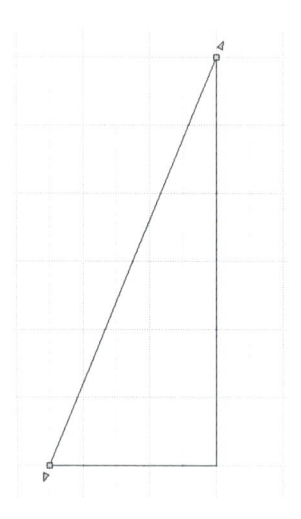

Figure 1

Appendix B

MathPro

One of the most useful tools that is included in your first quarter ITT Technical Institute instructional materials is the MathPro software package. This software is an invaluable tool for acquiring the mathematical skills that you will need to succeed in the Problem Solving course. In addition to offering an abundance of problems on which you may practice, MathPro contains short instructional video clips for each topic. These mini-lectures are given by the author of the mathematics portion of your Problem Solving Tools book, K. Elayn Martin-Gay.

Because accessing a particular program on the computer is discussed in your Introduction to Computers course, our focus here is on using the software. Once you have opened the software, click on the chapters button on the toolbar to see the following screen:

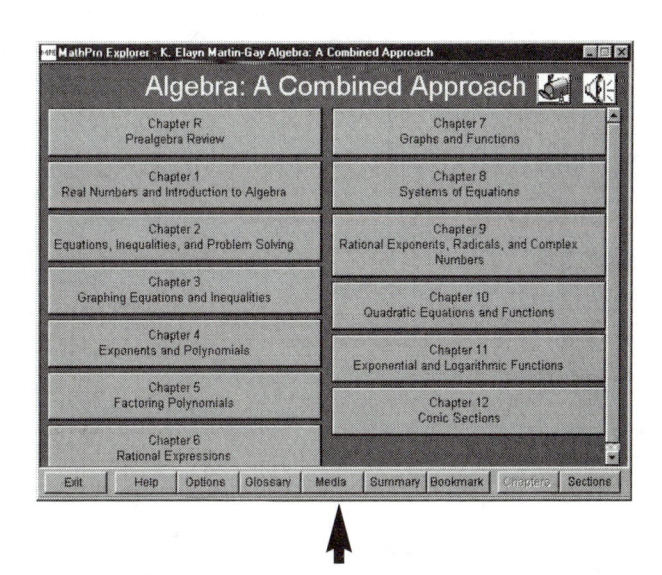

This screen is organized by the chapter titles from Part V of your Tools book. The numbering scheme for the software matches the chapters, subsections, and objectives of your book. If you look at the bottom of the window, you will find a button labeled "media." When you click this button, a listing of the video clips included in the software appears in a smaller window.

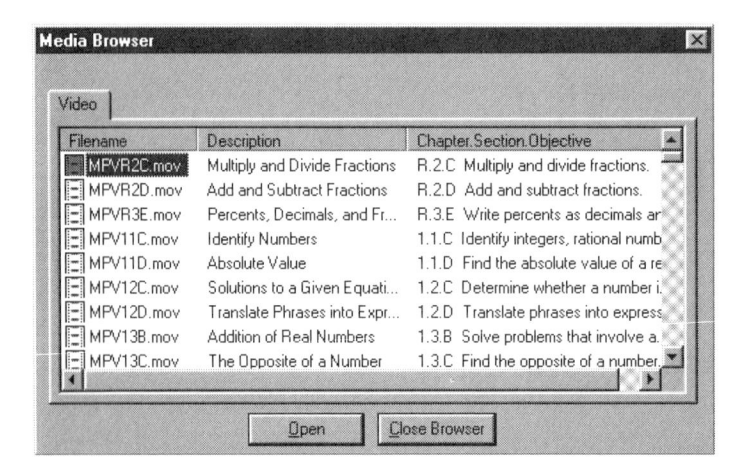

With your instructor's guidance this term, you will be directed to view specific video clips that may help you in solving a particular Thought Project.

Another important aspect of the software is the algorithmically generated problem sets that may be worked in a number of different modes. You may choose to view a worked-out example before trying a given problem; or you may receive step-by-step assistance with detailed explanations of the math concept under study. As an example, examine a beginning mathematical concept that will allow you to focus on learning the software itself.

Suppose that while solving a problem, you determine that using mathematics is the best problem solving strategy. However, to use the strategy effectively, you must be comfortable adding, subtracting, multiplying, and dividing signed numbers; recognizing that your skills in this area are rusty, your turn to MathPro. By looking at the introductory MathPro screen, you see that this topic is discussed in Chapter 1. When you click on the Chapter 1 button, the following window appears:

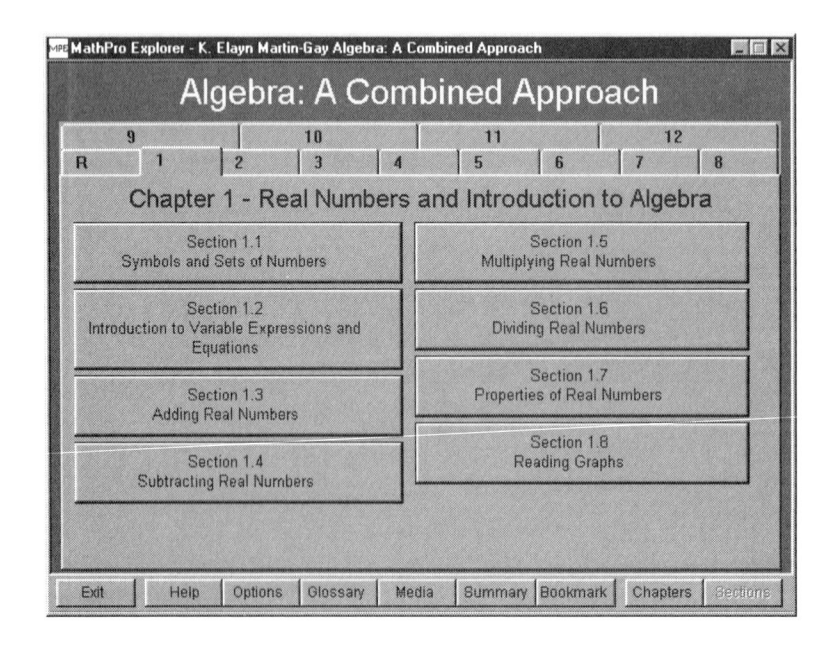

The information on the screen shows that real numbers are covered in several sections, 1.3, 1.4, 1.5, and 1.6. By subdividing the topics, you may focus on learning each new mathematical concept independently. Click on an individual section to study a given subtopic. Notice, that if you click on the media button, the numbering of the video clips corresponds to the chapters and sections from the Tools book.

If you have not already done so, it would be a benefit to become familiar with the MathPro software package. A good place to begin is by watching the Introduction to MathPro video that may be accessed by clicking on the "loud speaker" icon on the chapter menu screen.

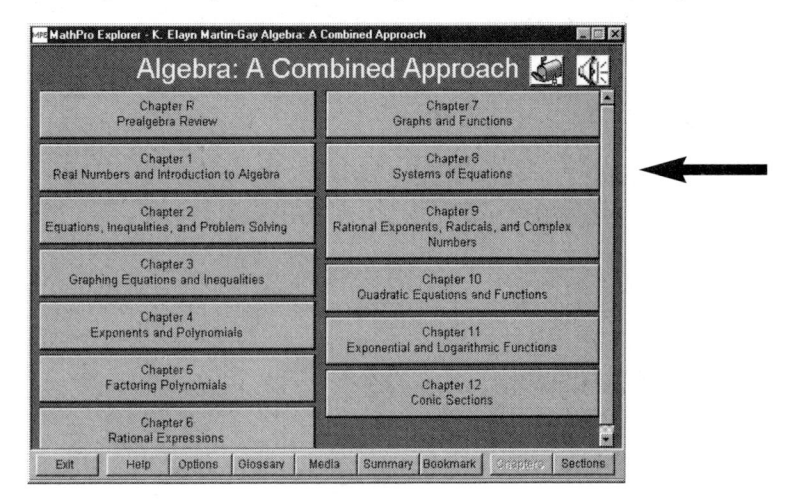

In addition to being a powerful support element for this course, MathPro is a software package that can help you throughout your entire technical career.

Glossary

Absolute zero—the lowest temperature that is possible in the universe.

Adenine—one of the four organic bases that are contained in a strand of DNA.

Alternating current—electrical current that changes direction with a regular frequency.

Archimedes' Principle—equation which states that the buoyant force exerted by a fluid on an object is proportional to the amount of fluid displaced by the object.

Area—the amount of two-dimensional space occupied by a shape.

Atom—basic building block of matter. All atoms contain a central region, or nucleus, with electrons surrounding it.

Base—in mathematics, the term to which the exponent is attached. It is the number, or variable, that is to be multiplied by itself.

Beat—a musical pulse.

Binomial—a mathematical expression that contains two terms.

Calorie—the unit of heat.

Capacitive reactance—a property of capacitors when wired in alternating current circuits. Because the electric field inside the capacitor changes when the current changes direction, there is an opposition to current flow.

Capacitive time constant—found by multiplying the resistance and capacitance together in an RC circuit, it is the amount of time required for the current to drop to 37% of its initial value.

Capacitor—an electronic device that stores electrical potential energy in its electric field.

Celsius scale—temperature scale based upon the freezing point and boiling point of water. 0° is defined as the point at which water freezes, and 100° is the point at which water boils.

Circuit—a complete path that allows for the flow of electric current.

Cloning—process by which an organism is reproduced from genetic information contained in its DNA.

Computer Icon—symbol on a computer screen that represents a file that can be accessed.

Conduction band—narrow region of energies of electrons that are free to move in a material.

Conductivity—a measurement of how easily electricity flows through a material.

Conductor—a material that allows for a large flow of electric current.

Continuity Equation—an equation that relates the velocity of a moving fluid to the cross-sectional area through which it is moving.

Cosine function—in a right triangle, the ratio of the length of the adjacent side to the length of the hypotenuse.

Coulomb—unit of electric charge.

Cytosine—one of the four organic bases that are contained in a strand of DNA.

Deoxyribonucleic Acid (DNA)—molecule that contains an organism's genetic information.

Deoxyribose—the sugar molecule that helps to form the backbone of the DNA molecule.

Desktop—the default computer screen with software *icons*.

Denominator—the bottom of a fraction.

Density—the ratio of the mass of an object to its volume.

Direct current—electrical current that flows in one direction only.

Displacement Equation—equation that is used to calculate the location of a moving object.

Drag—air resistance exerted on an object. The drag increases with the velocity of the object.

Electric current—the flow of electrical charges in a circuit.

Electricity—all of the phenomena associated with the interactions between and the movement of electrical charges.

Electromagnetic wave—a wave composed of an electric and magnetic portion. It has a characteristic frequency and wavelength, and travels at the speed of light.

Electron—a subatomic particle possessing negative electric charge that orbits the nucleus of an atom.

Element—a substance that is composed of atoms all of which have an identical number of protons in their nucleus.

Empirical—based on observations.

Energy—the ability of a system to execute work in changing its state.

Equation—a mathematical sentence that states that two different appearing quantities actually have the same value.

Exponent—a number that is placed in the top right hand corner of a term. It tells how many times the term is supposed to be multiplied by itself.

Exponential—an expression containing *e*, the base of the natural logarithms.

Factor—a term that can be evenly divided into a mathematical expression.

Factoring—process by which an expression can be broken into a sequence of terms. If these terms are multiplied together, they reproduce the original expression.

Fahrenheit scale—temperature scale on which water freezes at 32° and boils at 212°.

Farad—the unit in which the capacitance of an object is measured, where the capacitance is a measurement of the object's ability to store potential energy in its electric field.

Fiber optics—study of the materials that are used to carry information in the form of light signals.

Genetics—the study of hereditary information and its transmission.

Global warming—an increase in earth's surface temperature resulting from the build-up of atmospheric gases that will not allow excess heat to exit back into space.

Graph—a picture that summarizes quantitative information.

Gravitational acceleration—the acceleration that a falling object experiences because of the gravitational field generated by the planet.

Guanine—one of the four organic bases that are contained in a strand of DNA.

Half-life—amount of time required for a radioactive substance to decay to one half of its original mass.

Heat—energy associated with the motion of atoms and molecules in a material.

Helix—a spiraling geometric shape.

Hypotenuse—the side of a right triangle that is opposite the 90° angle.

Impedance—the opposition to current flow in an alternating current circuit.

Index of refraction—the ratio of the speed of light in a given medium to the speed of light in a vacuum. Using this number and Snell's Law, we are able to find the angle at which light will be bent as it moves between different materials.

Inductive reactance—in an alternating current circuit, it is opposition to current flow provided by the inductor. This opposition is due to the changing polarity of the magnetic field inside the inductor.

Inductor—an electronic device that stores potential energy inside of its magnetic field.

Insulators—materials that do not allow for a large current flow.

Isotope—the version of a particular element, determined by the number of neutrons inside the nucleus of the atom.

Junction—point in a circuit where the current divides.

Kelvin scale—absolute temperature scale. It is divided in the same increments as the Celsius scale, but uses absolute zero as its reference point.

Kepler's Law of Periods—law used to analyze the orbits of satellites. It relates the amount of time it takes the satellite to make one orbit to how far away the satellite is from the central mass it is orbiting.

Kinetic Energy—energy that an object possesses due to its motion.

Latent heat of fusion—for a material, a measurement of how easily the material moves between the solid and the liquid states.

Latent heat of vaporization—for a material, a measurement of how easily the material moves between the liquid and the gas states.

Lodestone—a natural form of magnet.

Logarithm—an alternative method of writing an expression that contains bases and exponents.

Magnet—type of material that attracts other types of materials such as iron.

Mass—the amount of matter contained in a physical body.

Measure—an increment of length in a musical score. Each measure is allowed to contain a certain number of *beats*.

Mole—a term of measurement similar to dozen. It is defined to be 6.02×10^{23} number of items.

Molecule—a stable object constructed by binding atoms together using the electromagnetic force.

Monomial—a mathematical expression containing only one term.

Nebula—a large mass of interstellar gas.

Neutron—an electrically neutral particle located inside the nucleus of atoms.

Newton's Law of Gravitation—law used to find the amount of gravitational attraction between two or more masses.

Node—point in a circuit at which the current divides.

Normal line—an imaginary reference line that is drawn perpendicular to a surface.

Note—a tone of definite pitch.

Nucleotide—the smallest piece of a DNA strand. It contains only one sugar, phosphate, and organic base.

Nucleus—the central, positively charged portion of an atom.

Numerator—the top portion of a fraction.

Ohmic losses—power losses that occur as the power is transmitted through lines that contain resistance.

Ohm's Law—equation that relates the voltage drop across a resistor to the current flow through the resistor and the resistance of the resistor.

Organic base—carbon-based molecule the sequence of which determines the genetic information in an organism.

Ozone—molecule that is composed of three oxygen atoms bound together.

Parallel wiring—when two circuit elements are wired in such a way that the current has an option through which element to flow.

Pascal's Principle—equation that relates the pressures in various portions of a container to one another.

Percentage—a fraction or ratio with 100 as the assumed denominator.

Period—the amount of time required for a physical system to return to its original configuration.

Phosphate—molecule contained in a strand of DNA that is composed of one phosphorous atom and four oxygen atoms.

Polarity—most commonly used in the study of electricity and magnetism, it refers to the orientation of the positive and negative terminals of a battery, or the orientation of the positive and negative poles in a magnet.

Polynomial—a mathematical expression containing more than one term.

Power—the rate at which the energy in a system is changing.

Power Wheel—pictorial representation of the relationship of power to other physical quantities such as voltage, current, etc.

Prefix—sequence of letters at the beginning of a word that alters its meaning.

Primary—in transformers, the starting voltage before it is modified by the transformer.

Proton—positively charged particle found in the nucleus of atoms. The number of protons inside the nucleus determines the *element*.

Pythagorean Theorem—equation that relates the lengths of the two legs of a right triangle to the length of the triangle's hypotenuse.

Radical—the root of a quantity.

Radiocarbon dating—archaeological dating technique based on the half-life of the carbon-14 isotope.

Ratio—the relative size of two quantities expressed as a fraction.

Refraction—process by which light is bent as it exits one material and enters another.

Resistance—opposition to current flow due to friction.

Resistor—electronic device that opposes current flow and in so doing dissipates energy in the form of heat.

Resonant frequency—in an alternating current circuit, the input frequency that yields the largest current flow.

Right triangle—triangle that contains a 90° angle.

Schematic—a pictorial representation of an electronic circuit.

Scientific notation—shorthand way of writing very large, or very small numbers.

Secondary—in transformers, the new voltage that has been changed from the *primary* by the *tranformer*.

Semi-conductor—material that conducts better than an *insulator*, but not as well as a *conductor*.

Series wiring—a method of wiring two or more circuit elements together such that all of the electric current that flows through one element also flows through the other.

Simultaneous equations—algebraic equations that can be solved using the same value of two or more variables.

Sine function—in right triangles, the ratio of the length of the opposite side to the length of the hypotenuse.

Snell's Law—equation that relates the angle of refraction that a light ray makes in one material to the angle of refraction that it makes in another material.

Step-down transformer—electronic device that takes the primary voltage and decreases it.

Step-up transformer—electronic device that takes the primary voltage and increases it.

Suffix—letter sequence attached to the end of a word that changes its meaning.

Supernova—the very powerful explosion of a star.

Tangent function—in right triangles, the ratio of the length of the opposite side to the length of the adjacent side.

Terminal velocity—the maximum speed that can be attained by a freely falling object.

Thymine—one of the four organic bases that are contained in a strand of DNA.

Total internal reflection—phenomenon in which light is not able to escape from a particular material and is reflected back inside the material.

Total resistance—the combined resistance of a sequence of resistors in a circuit.

Transformer—device which changes the voltages generated in an alternating current circuit.

Trinomial—mathematical expression containing three terms.

Unit—letters that are attached to a number giving guidance as to the type of physical quantity the number represents, i.e. length, time, etc.

Unit analysis—process of using the physical units in a problem to check for errors.

Universal Gravitational Constant—proportionality constant attached to Newtonian gravitation theory, 6.67×10^{-11} Nm^2/Kg^2.

Valence band—narrow range of energies of those electrons necessary to bind a solid.

Variable—a letter or symbol that represents an unknown number.

Velocity—the speed of an object with an associated direction.

Voltage—the electrical pressure that drives current flow.

Volume—the amount of three-dimensional space occupied by an object.

Wavelength—the length of one full cycle of a wave expressed in centimeters, inches, etc.

STRATEGIES FOR PROBLEM SOLVING WORKBOOK

REVISED PRINTING

BRIAN K. SALTZER

Pearson Custom Publishing

Cover art by Joe Black/Stock Illustration Source, Inc.

Copyright © 2000 by Pearson Custom Publishing.
All rights reserved.

This copyright covers material written expressly for this volume by the editor/s as well as the compilation itself. It does not cover the individual selections herein that first appeared elsewhere. Permission to reprint these has been obtained by Pearson Custom Publishing for this edition only. Further reproduction by any means, electronic or mechanical, including photocopying and recording, or by any information storage or retrieval system, must be arranged with the individual copyright holders noted.

Printed in the United States of America

10 9 8 7 6 5 4 3 2

Please visit our web site at www.pearsoncustom.com

ISBN 0-536-60907-1

BA 993023

PEARSON CUSTOM PUBLISHING
75 Arlington Street, Suite 300, Boston, MA 02116
A Pearson Education Company